COMING BACK TO EARTH

FROM GODS, TO GOD, TO GAIA

Lloyd Geering

EDITED WITH AN INTRODUCTION BY TOM HALL

POLEBRIDGE PRESS
Salem, Oregon

Cover and interior design by Robaire Ream

Library of Congress Cataloging-in-Publication Data

Geering, Lloyd, 1918-
Coming back to earth : from gods, to God, to gaia / Lloyd Geering ; edited with an introduction by Tom Hall.
    p. cm.
 Includes index.
 ISBN 978-1-59815-016-2
1. Christianity--21st century. 2. Christianity--Forecasting. 3. Postmodernism--Religious aspects--Christianity. 4. Christianity and culture. 5. Secularism. I. Hall, Tom, 1932- II. Title.

BR121.3.G43 2009
270.8'3--dc22

2009036144

TABLE OF CONTENTS

PREFACE

Between 2001 and 2008 I delivered a number of lectures in response to requests from the Westar Institute (Santa Rosa, California), St. Andrew's Trust for the Study of Religion and Society (Wellington, New Zealand), and the New Zealand Sea of Faith Network. At the time I regarded these lectures (or series of lectures) as independent compositions, and that is why an occasional expression or quote may appear more than once in this book. Not until my friend and very efficient editor Tom Hall drew my attention to the fact, did I realize that when read in chronological order of composition, these lectures constitute a distinct unity. Some years earlier I had similarly made the unexpected discovery that three of my already published books also formed a natural trilogy.

No doubt the reason for these discoveries is that the same themes were occupying my attention over a period of years, and each time I wrote or lectured I developed them a little bit further. As I explained in my recent autobiography *Wrestling with God* (2006), for over forty years (first as a parish minister for thirteen years, then as a theological teacher for sixteen years, and finally as a Professor of Religious Studies in a secular university for twelve years) it has been my continuing concern to find the most convincing way of relating the Christian tradition to the modern secular world.

As a theological student I was fortunate to be taught Church History by Helmut Rex, a refugee from Nazi Germany. Starting with a lecture on the philosophy of history he engendered in me a love of the subject that I had not previously had. I began to understand Christianity as a living tradition that has evolved and changed, and I now see that any religious tradition that becomes static has already begun its death throes. Of course, it took many years for me to understand the full significance of this valuable insight, and for quite some time I defended the credal structure of Christian orthodoxy as if that were an unchangeable essence.

In the forties and fifties I was able to do this the more readily because the liberal Protestant theology of about 1880–1950 was already rapidly accommodating itself to our new and more secular understanding of the world we live in. Indeed, it was my attempt in the sixties to make some small contribution to this ongoing process that involved me in the New Zealand theological controversy that came to a climax in the so-called heresy trial of 1967. Although acquitted of the charges laid against me—teaching false doctrine and disturbing the peace of the church—I nevertheless found that my efforts bore little immediate fruit. The mainline churches simply continued in the path advocated by my accusers, while I found myself regarded by many in the churches as a maverick who had departed from the Christian way.

In my view they had it back to front, for while most in the churches seemed to be anchored to a past that was fast becoming outdated, I was endeavoring to be faithful to the Christian path of faith as it moved into a radically changing future. I know this statement sounds very like the claim of the proud mother who exclaimed loudly, as she watched her son marching by in a procession, "Goodness! They're all out of step except my Johnnie!"

Nonetheless, I have come to the conclusion that, by and large, the reason for the now rapid decline of the mainline churches in the Western world is that they are "all out of step" with the modern secular world. The reason for this is not so much the supposed renegade behavior of the secular world as the failure of the church to take the next challenging steps in its four thousand year old path of faith. Whereas Abraham is said to have left his idols behind to go out into the unknown by faith alone, the churches (paradoxical though it may seem) reveal a lack of faith and insist on retaining the support of an infallible Bible and a set of unchangeable doctrines tailored to a worldview that has become obsolete.

Jesus is said to have warned his followers not to become "blind guides", as he judged the scribes to be, but that is what the churches are in great danger of becoming. Instead of continuing to walk the ever-changing path of faith from Abraham onwards, the churches have put their trust in idols that they have accumulated on the way and have become blind to the cultural situation they have now entered. This prevents them from seeing that the modern secular world, far from being the enemy of Christianity, is the legitimate continuation of the Judeo-Christian path of faith in the modern era. The modern global and secular world has emerged out of Western Christendom; moreover, in doing so it has increasingly though yet incompletely manifested Christianity's central doctrine—the Incarnation, the enfleshment of "God" in the human condition. God has indeed come down to earth!

This is the constant and developing theme of this series of lectures. I am grateful to Tom Hall for his suggestion that they be published as one book and to Polebridge Press for responding to his suggestion.

Lloyd Geering

INTRODUCTION

Not long ago I treated my adult study group at First Unitarian Church of Providence to the DVD of "The Secular Trinity," Lloyd Geering's address to the Westar Institute's 2001 Spring Conference. The powerful impression it made found dramatic expression in the surprise and outrage of a feisty 94-year-old lady who is a devoted long-time member. Upon learning that the speech was given eight years ago, she exclaimed, "Well, why are we just now learning of these things?"

Her challenge made me feel a bit remiss: should this viewing have preceded our examination of Brandon Scott on the parables, Bob Fortna on Matthew's gospel, Nigel Leaves' *The God Problem* and Richard Holloway's "The Wound of Religion"? No, for surely the failure to "get the word out" rests primarily with the clergy and their congregations! Instead of being forthright they have for years engaged in a conspiracy of silence in order to avoid facing the results of new knowledge in the wider culture as well as in biblical and religious scholarship. In short, the church has been stonewalling both intellectual trends and specific discoveries that challenge its traditional teachings.

Here it should be noted that my friend Alma (who at the end of our session handed me a blank check and asked me to order a copy of the DVD that she could send to her daughter and granddaughter—Alma is a nourisher indeed!) has for many years been a faithful Unitarian. And in my limited experience members of Unitarian-Universalist congregations have often finessed the problem of standard-brand Christianity's inability to make sense in the modern world by the simple expedient of abandoning those doctrines and practices they see as specifically Christian. The use of scripture has likewise fallen into such disuse that along with others in the group, my youthful-spirited nonagenarian repeatedly expresses surprise at the wonderful stories and deep wisdom to be found in both the Hebrew and Christian canons.

Liberal and Progressive Christians—of whom retired Episcopal Bishop John Shelby Spong and Marcus Borg are among the best-known examples—occupy a middle ground. Like Lloyd Geering they are aware that the obsolete sky-dwelling God of the Bible needs to be reimagined and that much of the traditional belief system is desperately out of place in modern Western culture, but they find inspiration in the message of that justly famous Galilean teacher and in the writings of the prophets and sages on whose insights he built.

Alas, much of the Christian church has in effect denied the existence of the problem and is consequently stuck in an embarrassing time warp. Despite all we have learned about the world from Galileo, Darwin, and Freud—and about religion from contemporary theologians and biblical scholars—they insist on claiming to believe in the three-tiered universe of the ancients, its otherworldly absentee Creator who is both a loving father and an occasional promoter of genocide, and a resuscitated Savior who was and is the only true son of that conflicted deity.

But they are swimming against the tide. The evolutionary biologist Stuart Kauffman, though a highly spiritual person, has correctly declared the idea of a "supernatural god" obsolete. Theologian Don Cupitt adduced the "intellectual muddle" and "disastrous . . . misreading of Jesus at the very center of Christianity" in his address "Reforming Christianity" delivered to the same conference that heard Lloyd define his secular trinity. One of Jack Spong's many fine books bears the title *Why Christianity Must Change or Die*. And not long after his challenging *Christianity Without God* was published, Lloyd Geering followed it with a series of lectures for St Andrew's Trust entitled "Is Christianity Going Anywhere?" His eloquent answer to this provocative question (it is, he predicted, but only if it is able to reinvent itself) soon appeared in a booklet and now appears as the second of his five public declamations that constitute this volume.

I can't recall precisely how the idea for this collection came about, but I remember awaking in the middle of the night with an inchoate but unshakable conviction that what I had heard that afternoon was the culmination of decades of thinking and writing by one of the world's most creative theologians. My friend Noel

Cheer of the New Zealand Sea of Faith Network had sent me a CD of Lloyd's keynote address to the group's yearly meeting in November 2008. It was a bravura performance in which the cleverly understated exposition and the visceral impact of its radical message combined to produce one of those "Yesss!" moments that forever change one's view of the world.

Mind you, I was not surprised. I had some years earlier been overwhelmed by the erudition and synthetic vision Lloyd displayed in his impressive trilogy: *Christian Faith at the Crossroads* (a 2001 re-publication of his 1980 volume, *Faith's New Age*); *The World To Come* (1999); and *Tomorrow's God* (2000). They too had provided a number of transformative insights. And thus when the redoubtable Char Matejovsky of Polebridge Press asked me to edit his forthcoming *Christianity Without God*, I was at once incredulous at my good fortune, uneasy at the prospect of emending text for so great a scholar, and fascinated by the implications of his argument.

I particularly recall two things about that experience. First, I was able to work directly from the edited manuscript to deliver a series of six sermons that were very well received by the congregation of a small rural church I was then serving as lay pastor. Second, and more important in the present context, it struck me that this ground-breaking book amounted to a synopsis of the major themes of the trilogy I had found chock-a-block with inspiring new insights.

And even as it was being written, Geering challenged us Westar conferees with "The Secular Trinity." It is therefore not surprising that just as that lecture reverberates with thoughts that went into the book, a subsequent lecture series—"Is Christianity Going Anywhere?" (2004)—both flows out of it and provides a hint of what was soon to follow. For since it was already clear that Geering was deeply concerned with the growing ecological crisis and the promotion of "green consciousness," it was natural that in "The Greening of Christianity" (2005) he should turn to an examination of how the Christian path of faith was rooted in the natural world and how its future prospects might be enhanced by creating "greener" forms of spirituality.

His next series, "In Praise of the Secular" (2007) picked up a subordinate but repeated theme from earlier addresses: the growing secularity of this increasingly global world of ours. The result was this carefully argued rejection of supernaturalism and eloquent advocacy of a radically "this-worldly" understanding of reality.

Whether or not he was consciously aware of the trajectory apparent in these works, his address to the 2008 New Zealand Sea of Faith conference, "God, Gaia, and Us," completed its earthward arc. For here the insights and motifs he had been developing for the better part of a decade came together in what he calls "a new form of mysticism." It is, of course, a radical form of realism, for it calls upon people of all faiths to complete the work of the Second Axial Age by bringing the sacred back home to the earth from whence, in the wake of the First Axial Age, the Judeo-Christian tradition had banished it to an imaginary heavenly realm.

If contemporary Christians find this proposal unpalatable, I suggest they recall what the scholars of the Jesus Seminar considered one of Jesus' most authentic voiceprints: the parable of the Leaven (Matthew 13:33 / Luke 13:20–21). In it we are assured that the promise of God's Kingdom will be realized only when the sacred and the profane are one—when the theophanic three measures of flour are thoroughly blended with the sacramentally impure leaven that represents secular human life.

And those concerned with holding fast to ritual and doctrinal orthodoxy (even at the cost of abandoning the common-sense reality of the world we now live in) should recall that Jesus' primary command, repeated in various forms, was to love—that is, to give freely of oneself to others. In walking the path of faith, he insisted, one's ultimate duty is to be fulfilled here on earth; and however difficult to perform, its definition is utterly simple and down to earth: "Treat others as you wish to be treated."

Or if you prefer your moral injunctions in verse, try this:

If you get more than you give,
One brief lifetime you will live;
But give more than you take away,
And taste eternity today.

Or if that seems to lack the correct secular tone, consider the down-to-earth profundity of a faith statement I saw on the back of a truck in Wellington: "Being nice to one another is the rent we owe for living on this lovely planet." Surely Gaia would smile.

Tom Hall

CHAPTER

1

THE SECULAR TRINITY

We are here to discuss the faith of the future and discern how
it is linked with the faith of the past. We are rightly using
the term "faith" rather than "religion" or even "Christianity," for
these latter terms have become too objectified. As Wilfred Cantwell
Smith showed in 1962 in *The Meaning and End of Religion*, it is a
modern and quite misleading practice to think of religion in general, and Christianity in particular, as objective things. He urged us
to turn back to the concept of faith. "Faith" is a much more universal term. It refers to the personal attitude of trust and hope that we
humans manifest as we both interpret the world in which we live
and respond to its demands.

Faith is an essential component of the human condition. We may
have only a little faith or we may have great faith, but without faith
of some kind we do not live as humans. During their respective
lifetimes each person and each community may be said to walk a
path of faith. Along each path the inner experience of faith comes
to expression in all sorts of external forms and structures such as
myths, rituals, holy writings, theological systems, moral codes,
social institutions, and so on. These objective data reflect the social
and cultural environment through which the path is moving, and
consequently they are diverse and also subject to change. For all
of these external objects that develop along a path of faith Smith
coined the term "the cumulative tradition." He warned us against
the danger of identifying faith with the cumulative tradition or any
part of it. Doctrines, rituals and other religious institutions are not
the content of faith; they are the products of faith and they serve
as markers of the particular path that certain people of faith have
trodden. To regard any of these markers as the object of faith is to
fall into the error of idolatry.

WALKING THE WALK

Christianity is a general term referring to a particular path of faith.
It is only one of several major paths that humans have trodden,
though for a long time Christians regarded it as the only true path

1

and referred to it simply as "the faith." This path originated long before the man Jesus, whose title, "the Christ," it now bears. Jesus himself spoke of faith as that which makes us whole and healthy. From what we can gather, Jesus was very much aware that he was walking on a path of faith that stretched back not only to Abraham but even to Adam.

During the last four thousand years of what we may call the Judeo-Christian path of faith, each new generation of people has learned from the preceding generation how to live by faith. The particular beliefs and practices of the cumulative tradition by which faith has been expressed have changed greatly in the course of time. Abraham, Jeremiah, Jesus of Nazareth, Augustine, Aquinas, and Luther were all people of faith who walked along that path, but the words and deeds in which they expressed their faith varied tremendously. As the cumulative tradition progressed, therefore, some elements dropped out of sight, new elements appeared, and many things changed.

Not long after the ancient Israelite prophets gave the path its initial direction, it underwent a considerable shift of emphasis during the Babylonian Exile, partly because it came under the influence of the Zoroastrian path of faith emanating from Persia. That is when Judaism and the institution of the synagogue came to birth. Some centuries later the influence of Jesus of Nazareth resulted in a radical change of direction from within, and as a result the Jewish path soon divided into two, and somewhat later into three branches— the Jewish, Christian, and Islamic paths.

During the first five centuries of the Christian era, Christian thinkers from Paul onwards set out to clarify the character of the new path of faith. Of necessity they were much influenced by the Greco-Roman culture in which they lived, but at the center of their thinking was the continuing influence of memories of Jesus, who was now worshipped as the Christ. They constructed the framework of thought and practice that shaped the Christian path of faith for the next fifteen hundred years. For simplicity they expounded this in the great creeds, and these received the stamp of authority from a succession of ecumenical councils, of which Nicaea was the first.

A TALE OF TWO CONFERENCES

Some noteworthy parallels can be seen between this present conference and the Council of ancient Nicaea. Of course they also exhibit major differences. We are not under the dominating chairmanship of the Emperor Constantine, who was bent on achieving a unified statement to be used to uphold and promote imperial power. Nor are we the official representatives of the many church bodies into which the once great universal church has now become fragmented. If we represent anybody at all, it is an anonymous host of genuine enquirers who value the Christian spirituality of the past, but who wonder where the path of faith is now leading.

The chief parallel between Nicaea and this Conference is this: the Christian thinkers of the first centuries lived in the religiously fluid aftermath of the Axial Period, while we live in the equally fluid and uncertain aftermath of the Second Axial Period. Let me explain. The term "Axial Period" is now widely used to refer to a time of radical cultural and religious changes that occurred between about 800 and 200 BCE. That period gave rise both directly and indirectly to those paths of faith that are today known as "the World Religions."

These new paths were pioneered by prophets, philosophers, and teachers who dared to subject their cultural past to critical examination. Prior to the Axial Period faith consisted of following meticulously in the footsteps of one's tribal ancestors. From the Axial Period onwards, however, faith called for some degree of self-critical reflection and personal commitment. Furthermore, each of these new post-Axial paths transcended the exclusively ethnic limitations of the cultural traditions of the past. They did so by enunciating sets of principles or ideas that had the potential to unite all humankind in a common path of faith. In this respect the Buddhist, Christian, and Islamic paths have been the most widely successful in crossing ethnic boundaries.

The Second Axial Period occurred in the Christian West between 1400 and 1900, with the Enlightenment marking a threshold of no return. Having reached its fullest flowering in the High Middle Ages, the Christian path of faith initiated a second period of radical questioning that gave rise to the modern, global, and secular world.

Both Axial Periods necessitated radical changes in the way faith was experienced, understood, and expressed in words. This may be illustrated by the changes that took place in understanding a basic religious concept—that of god. This concept originated in the pre-Axial Period, where it was created to explain the mysterious forces of nature that were perceived to dominate human existence. The gods (and other spirits) came to be conceived as an unseen order of spiritual beings who operated behind and through all visible phenomena, and who ultimately controlled human destiny.

THE OLD ORDER CHANGETH

During the Axial Period, however, the reality of these gods was questioned. The Israelite prophets iconoclastically rejected them as having no substantial reality. Plato and the Hindu seers, in their respective ways, saw the gods as ephemeral reflections of a deeper and unfathomable reality. The Buddha simply ignored them as irrelevant to the path of faith. But whereas the Buddhist path of faith thereafter abandoned the use of the god concept altogether, the Jewish, Christian, and Islamic paths retained the term but began using it in a radically new way. The Jews treated the plural word "gods" (elohim) as a singular, the Holy One, a term translated by Muhammad as al-Wahid. This god was quite different from the gods it replaced. As the ban on graven images makes clear, this god was beyond being visualized or objectified.

What has been too often overlooked is the fact that whereas each of the former gods had a special name and function, the new singular use of the word god left it without any specific meaning or content. That is why, in Biblical usage, we find frequent reference to "the god of . . ."—as in "the god of Abraham," "the god of Israel," "the god and father of Jesus Christ," "my god," and "your god," and so on. This implied that if you wish to know anything more about, say, "the god of Abraham," then you must look at the path of faith that Abraham walked and see what were his values and goals. That is the only way to know the character of "the God of Abraham." In other words, the God of Abraham consists of whatever motivated Abraham along his path of faith.

This further explains why the word "God" came to mean different things to different people. Jews, Christians and Muslims are all said to be monotheists—that is, they all believe there is only one God. And yet they do not worship the same God. To Jews, for example, God is the one who brought their forefathers out of Egypt, gave them the Torah and led them to the land of Promise. To Muslims, Allah is the one who revealed his Will to Muhammad in the Qur'an. To Christians, God means the One who became incarnate in Jesus of Nazareth.

A NEED FOR CREED

The difference between the Jewish God and the Christian God is made abundantly clear by the creeds of the early Christian centuries. During this formative period those who followed the Christian path of faith abandoned the pure monotheism of Judaism (later to be revived by Islam) and after much debate and no little dissension replaced it with the twin doctrines of the Incarnation and the Holy Trinity. They were affected by a number of influences, including even ideas from Zoroaster and Plato, but the chief ingredients of these twin doctrines were three areas of their experience they believed to be vital:

First was the inheritance from their Jewish origins of the oneness of God. This of course was pure monotheism and was expressed in the formula, "I believe in One God the Father Almighty, Maker of heaven and earth, and of all things visible and invisible." But this is not where the Creed stopped. In a second step, the Creed proceeded to modify this form of theism quite radically in the light of what they had inherited from the apostles—namely, the influence of the man Jesus of Nazareth. His felt presence, his deeds, and his teaching were believed to radiate the divine in such a way that this man had to be incorporated into their understanding of God. The way they did this is called the doctrine of the Incarnation. It was expressed particularly in the words "and was made man" and became by far the longest section of the Creed. To this was added a third element. They experienced an inner vitality at work within the fellowship of the church. This they called the Holy Spirit, or power of God within human minds.

The doctrine of the Holy Trinity attempted to preserve the unity of God while doing justice to these three experiences. The doctrine of the Incarnation bridged the gulf between divinity and humanity that existed in both polytheism and pure theism. By affirming both the divinity and the humanity of Jesus of Nazareth, the ancient Christian thinkers found a daring way of building humanity itself into the content of the God symbol.

These twin doctrines, finalized by the fifth century, served the Christian path of faith very well for the next 1000 years. Although they were never anything more than humanly devised formulas, they came to be used as sacred mantras like the one found in the hymn known as St. Patrick's Breastplate:—"I bind unto myself today the strong name of the Trinity." They were treated as divinely revealed truths and tended to be taken more and more literally. What started as the personae or masks of the invisible and non-objective deity came to be perceived as personalized and objectified. God the Father was even referred to as the Supreme Being—a personal being—for whom God was now the proper name. Then came the visual representations, starting with the icons and images of Jesus and the Virgin Mary. This process reached its climax when Michelangelo at last transgressed the ancient prohibition of the visualizing of God and painted a portrait of God the Father on the ceiling of the Sistine Chapel.

A TANGLED WEB UNRAVELS

This was on the eve of the Second Axial Period, and it may justifiably be seen as symbolic of how, by the High Middle Ages, Christian orthodoxy had over-reached itself. The whole framework of Christian thought constructed in the first five centuries thereafter began to disintegrate. The Renaissance, the Protestant Reformation, and the Enlightenment followed in quick succession. The doctrines of the Incarnation and Trinity, as traditionally understood, came under strong criticism. Diversity and confusion resulted and the unity they had provided for the Christian path of faith was increasingly on the ebb.

In place of the doctrine of the Holy Trinity, a non-Trinitarian theism began to appear at one pole of thought and atheism at the other, with deism, pantheism, and panentheism at various points in between. Indeed, the most vigorous defenders of Christian orthodoxy today are theists rather than true trinitarians. The ancient Gnostic heresy of Docetism, which asserted that Jesus was a divine figure who only appeared to be human, finally prevailed in much popular Christian devotion. As a result, Jesus' humanity was largely lost sight of, and the short life of the human Jesus was almost completely replaced by the figure of Christ, the glorified Son of God sitting at the right hand of God the Father. In short, the daring and paradoxical character of the Incarnation and the Trinity has been largely lost in traditional Christianity.

It is tempting to conclude, as many do, that the doctrines of the Incarnation and the Trinity are now outmoded and should be discarded. I wish to suggest rather that what should be discarded is the way these doctrines had come to be understood on the eve of the Second Axial Period, the event that brought about their undoing. Further I wish to suggest that, paradoxical though it may seem, it was the daring and innovative character of the doctrines of the Incarnation and of the Holy Trinity that eventually led to the Second Axial Period. Moreover, I contend that they constitute the reason why the modern secular world emerged in Christian Europe rather than elsewhere. Far from being judged to be obsolete and meaningless, then, these doctrines may be seen as having an unexpected new relevance in the global, secular world to which they have led.

RESTORING AN OLD FABRIC

The full humanity of Jesus is once again being acknowledged, thanks to the work of biblical scholars from Strauss to the Jesus Seminar. The recovered footprints and voiceprints of the historical Jesus show he was truly human in every way, even to being a man of his own times. This makes it necessary to look at the doctrine of the Incarnation in quite a new light, and it re-opens the question of why the pioneers of the Christian path of faith dared to incorporate humanity into the concept of God. To restrict the incarnation of the divine to one human person, namely the man Jesus of Nazareth, is to miss its full significance. The idea that God could become enfleshed even in one special person was more than most Jews could accept at the time, and so much so that all pure monotheists, such as Jews and Muslims, continue to reject it to this day.

And although the idea that God could become enfleshed in humanity as a whole is more than even most Christians have been able to accept, the seeds of this more extensive interpretation of incarnation were already present in the New Testament. Jesus was not at first separated from his fellow-humans by a great gulf in the same way the glorified Christ later became to be; rather he was seen as the one who had brought God down to earth. His teaching and manner of life enabled people to sense the presence of the divine in the affairs of ordinary daily life.

Even Paul spoke of Jesus as the representation or embodiment of the whole human race. Just as the first Adam (in Hebrew the word means "humankind") embodied the whole human race, so the Christ figure evolving out of Jesus was said to be the New Adam (i. e., the embodiment of the new humankind). "For as in Adam all die, so also in Christ shall all be made alive." That is why Paul spoke of all Christians as being "in Christ." They were conceived of as participating in the continuing incarnation.

Thus from the beginning and continuing in later hints, Christianity has long reflected the seed-thought that humanity itself was to be the enfleshment or incarnation of the divine. This is why it later became common to speak of the Christian life as one of "sanctification," and why the Eastern Orthodox Church speaks of the Christian life as the process of "deification." Even Aquinas said, "The Incarnation is the exaltation of human nature and consummation of the Universe."

The doctrine of the incarnation is therefore to be applied to the whole of humankind. David Strauss regarded the Incarnation of God in Jesus Christ not as a unique historical event, but as a symbolic portrayal of the spiritual process of the cosmos that has been in operation from eternity and consists of the humanization of God and the divinization of humankind.

The first modern theologian to expound at some length this way of understanding the Incarnation was Ludwig Feuerbach. This he did in his book *The Essence of Christianity*, wherein he contrasted "the False or Theological Meaning of the Incarnation" with "the True or Humanistic Meaning of the Incarnation." In Christian orthodoxy the humanity of Jesus had been taken up into heaven and lost in the Holy Trinity. For Feuerbach the Incarnation meant that the divine had come down to earth to reside permanently within humanity. Following the example of the New Testament declaration that "God is love," Feuerbach took the being of God to be nothing else but such moral values as love, justice, and compassion—qualities that henceforth were to be manifested within the human race. The doctrine of the incarnation spelled the end of theism, because the God whom theists had mythically ensconced upon a heavenly throne has now come down to dwell in human flesh—in <u>all</u> human flesh.

FASHIONING A NEW GARMENT

This means, first, that we humans must live without the divine heavenly props thought to exist in the past. As Jesus is reported to have said, "We must be mature as God is mature." Second, it means that we now have to play on earth the role that theism had assigned to an objective, supernatural god. Not only is the heavenly throne empty, but heaven itself is an empty void. As Feuerbach saw it, the incarnation, properly understood, marked a turning point in human history; yet not until that understanding had led to the Second Axial Period have we been able to recognize the fact. The emergence of the modern secular world is thus to be seen as the logical consequence of the doctrine of the incarnation and the legitimate continuation of the Judeo-Christian path of faith.

Feuerbach was so far ahead of his time that he was completely rejected and his insights lost sight of for more than a century. Yet he was not the only one to see a connection between the doctrine of the incarnation and the coming of the modern secular world. In 1889 Charles Gore (later Bishop of Oxford) edited a symposium of Essays on "The Religion of the In-carnation" called *Lux Mundi* (The Light of the World). They were written, he said, out of the conviction that the epoch in which he and their authors lived was "one of profound transformation, intellectual and social, abounding in new needs, new points of view, new questions,"—an epoch in which "theology must take a new course". One of the contributors, J. R. Illingworth, warned Christians not to regard secular thought as the enemy of Christianity, but as that which was correcting its falsehoods, saying, "Secular civilization has co-operated with Christianity to produce the modern world. It is nothing less than the providential correlative and counterpart of the incarnation."

On this side of the Second Axial Period, we in the secular world are in a position to appreciate, as people after the First Axial Period were not, that the cumulative tradition of each path of faith is a human creation. All human languages, all philosophies and doc-trines, and all religious concepts, such as the gods and God, are of human creation. The heavenly world was wholly a creation of the human imagination.

LEARNING A NEW LANGUAGE

As we now walk by faith into the future, we have to decide how much from the past path of faith we find useful and how much we must leave behind. For example, what are we to do with the concept of 'God'? Although the theistic use of the term has now become obsolete, that does not necessarily mean it has to be dis-carded any more than it had to be abandoned at the First Axial Period. Even though we must now acknowledge the symbolic character and human origin of this and other words and concepts, we will still need religious symbols with which to express our quest for spiritual fulfillment.

But if we continue to speak of god as people did during the first Axial Period, we must again learn to use the term in a radically new way. God is a symbolic word that originated in ancient mythology.

We use it to refer to whatever concerns us in an ultimate way, to use the well-known phrase of Paul Tillich. Even Martin Luther was aware of this, for he said, "faith and God have inevitable connection. Whatever your heart clings to and confides in, that is really your God." Don Cupitt put it this way: "God is the mythical embodiment of all that one is concerned with in the spiritual life." Similarly, Gordon Kaufman says, "The symbol of God claims to represent to us a focus for orientation which will bring true fulfillment and meaning to human life. It sums up, unifies, and represents in a personification what are taken to be the highest and most indispensable human ideals and values." Thus, if we continue to speak of God, we are pointing to the values, goals, and aspirations that motivate us to follow the path of faith.

The Christian thinkers of the first five centuries expressed their values and aspirations by speaking of their God as the Holy Trinity—Father, Son, and Holy Spirit. What motivates us on our path of faith? What are the highest values and aspirations to which we respond in faith?

To answer these questions we must acknowledge that the world we live in looks very different from the way it looked to the ancient Christian thinkers. People both before and after the First Axial Period felt they were surrounded by, and often in close touch with, a spirit world. Today, of course, we use the word "spirit" metaphorically, if we use it at all. Where they talked about spirit as the substance of reality, we talk about physical energy. Where they explained natural phenomena in terms of gods and spirits, we do so in terms of electrons, quarks, and nuclear forces. Where they explained living creatures as fleshly embodiments of spirit or of a life-principle, we talk of organisms that are identifiable by DNA and chromosomes, immune systems and amino acids. We see ourselves as human organisms who feel with our bodies and think with our brains and nervous systems.

O BRAVE NEW WORLD!

Since we are much more focused on the physical world than were the ancients, reality for us is what we can confirm with our senses and what is open to public investigation. All the rest—including religion, philosophy, and science—is human interpretation, and this remains open to continual review. Our reality consists of the physical universe and, compared with how people perceived it even up until only 200 years ago, this reality has expanded in time and space beyond the ability of our minds to contain it.

The universe is one enormous bundle of energy. This is the basic stuff of reality. We do not quite know what energy is, but we know a good deal about how it works. The universe is awe-inspiring, not only in its dimensions but also in its capacity to create out of itself ever more complex and beautiful patterns of energy. First came the "big bang," then the slow accumulation of gases into stars, then the explosions of supernovas into star dust, then the formation of planets out of star dust, and finally, to date, the evolution of life on at least one planet. The universe has been a continuing process of change, manifesting both growth and decay over some fifteen billion years. At any one moment the universe may appear to be a static changeless thing, but viewed in the dimension of cosmic time, it is dynamic and alive.

Although we speak of the universe as having had a beginning, there was never a time when it did not exist, for time and space themselves came into existence only with the universe itself. Therefore, the universe is all there is; nothing is outside of it and nothing came before it. As a result, it is now illogical to postulate the prior existence of a Creator. The universe has to be self-explanatory, and from the universe itself we must learn what it can tell us about itself and how it works.

Furthermore, we are not only in this universe but we are an integral part of it. Our very existence and our continuing life are dependent upon it. That is why our pre-Axial ancestors believed their destiny to be in the lap of the gods—one of whom was Mother Earth. And even today, in recognition of the fact that we are dependent on the processes of nature, we are still inclined to speak of Mother Nature, although now we are aware we are speaking meta-phorically. Moreover, the Christian path of faith has long sustained a thin line of mystical tradition, starting with the ancient Neo-

Platonists and continuing through such people as Jakob Boehme, Bruno, and Spinoza—all of whom identified Nature with the divine. Schelling (1775–1854) saw Nature as an infinite, self-developing super-organism that is realizing itself in finite matter and coming to consciousness though human consciousness.

Many of the processes of nature that ancient humans found awesome we readily explain in quite mundane ways; yet those phenomena have in turn been replaced in our new picture of the universe by other mysteries that are just as awe-inspiring. We know extremely little about what takes place in the rest of this universe. We have no idea, and we may never know, whether life exists anywhere else within it. We do know that life on our planet seems to have been evolving over some three billion years and that the human species emerged out of a myriad of evolving living species. It did so only very recently, relative to the story of the Earth, and more by accident than by any apparent design. There is no obvious reason why we have evolved as we have, or even why there should be any life at all on this planet. The origin and purpose of human existence (if indeed it has a purpose) remain a mystery.

BACK TO BASICS

Because we are so dependent on the physical universe as a whole and on this planet earth in particular, the natural world itself must be the first focus of our faith. In his later and lesser-known book, *The Essence of Religion* (1848), Feuerbach acknowledged this when he said, "that upon which human beings are fully dependent is originally nothing other than Nature. Nature is the first, original object of religion." The most pressing aspects of our dependence upon nature are very basic. They are largely the same as those we share with the other animals—the need for air, drink, food, shelter, survival, and the regeneration of the species. Built into every species, including humans, are the instincts to survive and to procreate. These basic needs and animal instincts were the starting-point from which our primitive human ancestors set out on their path of faith, slowly and unconsciously creating human culture. We too must go that far back. We are today relearning that the basic needs—pure air, clean water, healthy food, adequate shelter, the regeneration of the species, and the overcoming of all threats to human survival—have once again become the ultimate, and therefore the religious, issues to which we must "devote" ourselves.

It is not sufficient to acknowledge our dependence on the world. We have to learn to trust it—to put our faith in it—in much the same way as our Christian forbears put their faith in its supposed Creator. There is much about the world that fosters faith. It has an awe-inspiring capacity to produce order and design out of chaos, to create beauty, to bring forth life. We are afflicted by earthquakes, storms, and disease—what we call natural disasters; yet the changing seasons keep bringing renewal. The story of evolution itself is spellbinding. The beauty we see through the microscope is breathtaking. There is much about the world to inspire awe, to foster faith, and to renew hope.

No one has expressed this more dramatically than the devout Jesuit priest and scientist Teilhard de Chardin, who wrote, "If as the result of some interior revolution, I were to lose in succession my faith in Christ, my faith in a personal God, and my faith in spirit, I feel that I should continue to believe invincibly in the world. The world (its value, its infallibility and its goodness)—that, when all is said and done, is the first, the last and the only thing in which I believe. It is by this faith that I live. And it is to this faith, I feel, at the moment of death, rising above all doubts, I shall surrender myself."

When Teilhard spoke of his faith in the world, he was not referring merely to rocks and rivers, nor even less to atoms and electrons. To appreciate what he meant one needs to read his magnum opus *The Phenomenon of Man*, preferably at one sitting. This is one of the great spiritual classics of modern times. Here is an unfolding vision of the evolving universe in all of its breath-taking grandeur and awe-inspiring mystery. It is a vision of cosmic creativity on the grandest possible scale, surpassing any description of the glory of God written during the ages of theism.

Most impressive of all is the way Teilhard builds into his vision of the evolving universe two great thresholds of change. First came the transition on this planet from non-life to life, resulting in the emergence of the biosphere, similar to but distinct from the lithosphere, the atmosphere and the stratosphere. Then within the biosphere, but only in the species homo sapiens, came the transition from life to reflective thought, resulting in the emergence of the noosphere. Teilhard coined this term in 1925 to refer to the layer of self-critical thought covering the already existing layer of life, which in turn covered the inorganic lithosphere.

A THINKING UNIVERSE?

Such is the creativity present in the self-evolving universe that it has the potential not only to become alive, but also to think. This potential, Teilhard argued, must have been there from the beginning and present within the energy that constitutes the basic stuff of the universe. As energy organized itself into ever more complex patterns, so its potential for consciousness reached ever higher levels. In the growing self-consciousness of humankind the universe is becoming aware of itself. Our minds have become the mirror through which the universe sees and understands itself.

This whole new way of understanding reality is today's equivalent of the traditional doctrine of the Incarnation. It used to be said that the divine Creator Father had become incarnate in human flesh. Now, and on a much grander scale, we may say that cosmic creativity has enfleshed itself in the earthly species we call humankind. What is more, whereas cosmic creativity seemed to be blundering along blindly for eons without any clear purpose, it has now through the medium of human consciousness manifested itself in purposeful activity.

In the traditional doctrine of the Incarnation, the man Jesus was seen as the prototype of the new humankind, or the expression of the "new being," to use Paul Tillich's term. The subsequent elevation of the man Jesus to divine status, which took place in ancient Christian thought, may now be taken as a symbolic premonition of things to come. The verbal imagery of Jesus sitting on the right hand of God, wielding divine power and responsible for ultimate judgment, is a sobering parable of the grave responsibilities now coming to rest upon the shoulders of the human race. As Jesus was once assumed to be able to think with the mind of God, so on this particular planet the collective human mind is the organ of thought through which the universe can now direct the process of future evolution on this planet. Now that the human race is being forced increasingly to play the role of God with regard to the sustaining of earthly life, the doctrine of the incarnation, interpreted in this way, has taken on a striking new relevance for this global, secular, and ecological world.

IT AIN'T OVER 'TIL IT'S OVER

The evolving process is far from having reached an end. Indeed, mankind, as Nietzsche suggested, is an unfinished animal. And while many signs suggest that the evolving process is now accelerating, we have no guarantee of ongoing progress.

From the "big bang" to the present, what came forth at each step resulted from already existing potentials, but that does not mean that everything was predetermined. There was no necessity for potential possibilities to be realized. In fact, the majority of possibilities have either not been realized or have ended in blind alleys. But as the evolving process has proceeded, what Teilhard called a "cosmic drift" has taken place. As the level of consciousness rose, chiefly in the human species, the evolutionary process came to depend more on personal choices. On the one hand this made the future less predictable, but on the other it made possible a more purposeful future.

In the course of evolving to our present state of self-consciousness, we humans have come to recognize that we are only a tiny part of a self-evolving universe in which we are a self-evolving species. From one point of view we are a self-made species. For what makes us human is not our DNA, the majority of which we share with the other higher animals. What makes us human is what we have collectively created, including language, ideas, culture, knowledge, religion and science. All this is so much a part of what we are and what we live in that we have no particular name for it. It not only shapes the way we see reality but it also largely becomes the world in which we live. The philosopher Karl Popper called it World 3, to distinguish it from World 1 (the physical world) and World 2 (consciousness). World 3 is a human product, resulting from human reflection and creativity and mainly generated after the advent of the noosphere.

Consider some further interesting parallels between the traditional doctrine of the Incarnation and what is here being described. When the traditional doctrine of the Incarnation began to evolve in the first century, no clear distinction was at first made between the continuing influence of Jesus, the work of the Holy Spirit, and the mind of the church. Similarly, we find it difficult to distinguish between the human species and what the human species has collectively created; yet without World 3 we could not be human. This leads to a further oddity: because the content of World 3 developed differently in a variety of geographical areas, we have created different ways of being human—e. g., a Maori way, a Chinese way, a Christian way, a Muslim way, etc.

A GLOBAL MELTING-POT

As a result of the globalizing process that followed the Second Axial Period, all these different ways of being human are losing their absolute distinctiveness and a common way of being human is slowly emerging. This is coming about through the widening and maturing of human consciousness to what may be called global consciousness. This process is currently being fostered at an accelerating pace by the interchange of reliable knowledge, the traditional mass media of communication, and the Internet. Global consciousness is the modern equivalent of the Holy Spirit in the New Testament. We could well be living on the eve of an awe-inspiring new leap—a mutation—in the process of cosmic evolution. Unfortunately, we have no guarantee of this; for in fact we might be living in the last days before the human species brings about its own destruction.

As the primitive Christians looked into the future with faith based on their current experience, they expressed the substance of their faith in terms of the Holy Trinity of Father, Son, and Holy

Spirit. We in turn must draw on our basic experiences of reality to express our faith for the future.

A NEW TRINITY FOR
A NEW WORLD

Our experiences of reality are very different. Yet, strangely enough, they also lead to a trinity—what we may call a secular or this-worldly trinity. The first element is this self-evolving physical universe, which as we understand it, encompasses the whole of reality. Second is the human species that has evolved out of this creative universe and thereby brought us into existence. The third "being" is that which the collective consciousness of humankind has in turn brought forth—the body of cultural knowledge (earlier referred to as World 3) without which we could not be human. These three constitute the God "in whom we live and move and have our being."

In the traditional doctrine of the Trinity the ancient thinkers took great pains to keep the Father, the Son, and the Holy Spirit clearly distinguished from one another and at the same time to affirm their essential unity. So it is with us. We distinguish clearly between the physical universe and the human species that lives within it. We also distinguish clearly between ourselves and the body of cultural knowledge that we inherit from our predecessors and to which we in turn contribute. Yet these three are so essentially a single reality that they cannot exist in separation from one another.

As Father, Son, and Holy Spirit were proclaimed "three in one" because of the Incarnation, so the self-creating universe, the self-evolving human species and the emerging global consciousness are of one "substance" because of the cosmic creativity which manifests itself in all three. Clearly this understanding of the secular trinity owes much to the earlier affirmations of the Incarnation and of Holy Trinity. The more we humans become an harmonious global society, relating in a healthy way to one another and to the planet, the more confident we can be about the future. This hope rests upon putting our faith in the secular trinity of the world, humanity and global consciousness.

IS CHRISTIANITY GOING ANYWHERE?

2

CHRISTIANITY AT THE CROSSROADS

C hristianity stands today at a critical point in its long and complex history. Too few Christians recognize that humankind is moving into an increasingly global and secular future. Christianity and all other religions must now come to terms with this new global context. Not only are we becoming dependent on a global economy, but the many diverse cultures of the past are being drawn into a global cultural maelstrom. In the last four hundred years our view of the universe in which we find ourselves has changed out of all recognition; and so also has our understanding of culture, of religion, and of the human condition itself.

For some four or five centuries the advent of the modern secular world appears to have been eroding Christianity, at least in its classical form. With the gift of hindsight we can now say that the Protestant Reformation was the first sign of this. The Reformation fragmented the ecclesiastical structure within which the Christian tradition had always lived. The church had long been held to be an article of faith, as in the words of the Creed, "I believe in one, holy, catholic and apostolic church." The church saw itself as a divine institution founded by Jesus Christ, and it claimed to speak with finality on all matters of essential truth until challenged by the Protestant Reformers. The Reformation caused this "one, holy, catholic, and apostolic church" to break up into an increasing number of competing churches. Christians were left in a state of bitter hostility to one another as evidenced by the religious wars of the seventeenth century. As church structures became increasingly divided, they manifested just how human they are.

To replace the channel of divine authority once thought to be seated in the church, the Protestant churches were thrown back on the words of the Bible. The Bible was believed to reveal without error the origin of the world, the meaning of history, the moral laws by which all should live, and the only path to salvation. But in the nineteenth century this widespread confidence in the Bible was badly shaken, as biblical scholars began to study it with the modern tools of literary and historical criticism. The Bible, far from being

21

an infallible source of divinely revealed knowledge, proved, like the church, to be all too human in origin.

Just as the sixteenth century shattered the unity of the church, so the twentieth witnessed the progressive dissolution of traditional Christian doctrine. The recognition that the Bible was of human origin had serious consequences for the two most basic concepts in Christianity: the divinity of Jesus Christ, and the reality of God.

The traditional image of Jesus Christ began to disintegrate into a collage of history, myth and devout imagination. People came to recognize that the Jesus Christ worshipped in the Christian tradition, though initially based on the memories of the historical figure of Jesus, had long been shaped by the collective imagination and devotion of the Christian community.

At the same time, the theistic belief in God as the supreme personal being—a belief inherited from Judaism and basic to Christian orthodoxy from the beginning—was ceasing to win conviction. At the beginning of the twentieth century there were still only a few who dared to call themselves atheists. By the end of the century the traditional belief in God was declining rapidly. Even Christian theologians were beginning to abandon theism. Don Cupitt expounded what he chose to call a non-realist view of God, in which "God" becomes a symbolic term referring to our highest values and aspirations. Similarly, Gordon Kaufman wrote, "The symbol 'God' sums up, unifies, and represents in a personification what are taken to be the highest and most indispensable human ideals and values." Thus, belief in the reality of God, on which Christian orthodoxy has always depended, is today severely eroded. Catholic theologian Johann-Baptist Metz joined Lutheran theologian Jürgen Moltmann in declaring "a permanent constitutional crisis for theology". All of this I have discussed more fully in chapter 3 of *The World to* Come, "The Disintegration of Orthodoxy."

Even by the beginning of the twentieth century some discerning Christians were already sensing that Christianity was facing a crisis. Such a person was George Tyrrell (1861–1909), the leading Catholic Modernist in Britain. In his book, *Christianity at the Cross-roads* (1910), he defined a Modernist as "a churchman who believes in the possibility of a synthesis between the essential truth of his religion and the essential truth of modernity." But the Vatican was having none of it. Modernism was condemned; Tyrrell and other Catholic Modernists were excommunicated. Yet books with similar titles to that of Tyrrell continued to appear throughout the century. These are a few of them: *The Crisis of Faith* by Stanley Hopper *(*1947); *The End of Conventional Christianity* by Dutch Catholic W. H. van de Pol (1967); *Why Christianity Must Change or Die* by Bishop Jack Spong (1998). When my own *Faith's New Age* (1980) was republished in USA in 2001 it was retitled *Christian Faith at the Crossroads.*

COPERNICUS AND DARWIN

Why is Christianity facing this crisis? The first part of the answer lies in the way Copernicus and Galileo opened the door to what became our current view of the world as a space-time universe. The new Copernican cosmology led to more subtle and radical changes than even the church authorities who condemned Galileo were able to recognize at the time. Galileo brought the sun, moon, and stars into the same physical universe as the earth. In other words the heavens (or dwelling place of God) and the earth (or dwelling place of humans) have become parts of one and same physical reality. This was to have serious consequences for the traditional dichotomies of heavenly/earthly, supernatural/natural, and spiritual/material. The Copernican revolution was the first step in the emergence of the modern secular world, in which we see the universe operating according to its own internal laws. These laws operate even within living organisms, from the simple cell to the complex human organism. What our forbears took to be signs of supernatural forces turn out to be only the products of primitive interpretation and human imagination.

Since all educated persons throughout the earth, including even fundamentalist Christians, now share the space-age view of the universe, that does not in itself explain the crisis in Christianity. A second reason lies in the impact of Charles Darwin and the evolutionary account of the origin of all living species on this planet.

As the Copernican revolution displaced the earth from the center of the physical universe, the Darwinian revolution displaced the human species from its unique place among all species as that made in the image of god. Thus it is that fundamentalist Christians strongly reject Darwinism to this day. During the twentieth century, however, most thinking Christians largely absorbed the notion of biological evolution.

NEW AWARENESS OF HUMAN CULTURE

The real threat to Christianity has been something more subtle and more devastating than Darwinism. It has been the modern knowledge explosion. The cosmological revolution introduced by Copernicus was simply the first sign. The biological revolution advanced by Darwin was simply the second sign. What followed was the somewhat slower recognition that human culture itself has evolved. By "culture" I mean "a complex whole which, grounded in a common language, includes the knowledge and beliefs that constitute a particular world-view, along with a set of customs, morals, skills, and arts, with which to respond to that world." Culture is essential to our human condition. Only by being born into a culture and shaped by it do we become human. It is not our DNA alone that makes us human, for some 98% of it we share with the gorilla; it is also our culture that makes us human. Not only were we humans not created in our present form on the sixth day (as the Genesis account has it) but it took aeons of time for the human condition to evolve and it did so in tandem with the evolution of human culture. And unlike DNA, culture is something that the human species itself has collectively created.

From time immemorial our ancestors took human culture for granted, and most people still do. Being immersed from birth in culture, however primitive, people have been unaware of their dependence upon it. We have taken for granted language, the very basis of culture, much as we long took for granted the very air we breathe. People never used to think of language as something humanly created; it was assumed to have existed before the beginning of time. Indeed, in the biblical myth of origins, it was the very instrument by which the world was created. God had only to say, "Let there be light!" and there was light.

What made human culture possible was the evolution of human language. What made human language possible was the natural human ability to create symbols; the basis of language is the symbolization of sounds. Once we humans came to recognize that human languages and cultures have slowly evolved out of the primitive social life of our pre-human ancestors, it meant that we humans have, collectively, created language and culture. This has had the effect of turning our previous assumptions upside down. Human culture is the man-made environment of thought and meaning in which we live and move and have our being. We become human as we are shaped by the culture into which we are born. But we in turn help to shape the culture we pass on to the next generation.

Whether a proto-language and a proto-culture ever existed, we do not know. What we do know is that as the human species spread around the globe, it created thousands of languages, cultures, and subcultures. Each culture is an ever-evolving and developing continuum of words, stories, ideas, codes of behavior and social practices. It flows through time like an invisible ever-changing stream. In the past the many cultural streams flowed on in relative independence from one another, but today they are converging to form one global cultural sea. Indigenous peoples are not the only ones who face the prospect of losing their cultural identity. All cultures are today competing with one another; and at the same time they are contributing to the formation of a possible, and as yet incipient, global culture. The coming global culture will be humanly created just as all past and present cultures have been.

THE CUMULATIVE TRADITION

That which provides each culture with motivation, cohesion, and a vision of where it is going is what we may call its religion. Religion has been usefully defined as "a total mode of the interpreting and living of life." To be religious is to be deeply concerned with whatever matters most to us in life. It involves our highest goals and values. As the theologian Paul Tillich said, religion is the dimension of depth both in personal experience and in culture. The coming global culture will also have its religious dimension, but it will be experienced in secular terms. By "secular" I do not mean non-religious but "this-worldly and natural" as opposed to "other-worldly and supernatural."

Unfortunately, in popular usage, the word "religion" is too often identified with the division of the universe into the dichotomous realms of earthly/heavenly, natural/supernatural, and material/spiritual, so that one is thought to be religious only if one still believes in a supernatural, heavenly, spiritual world. That division has now become obsolete. What Copernicus did was to bring the heavenly bodies into the same physical realm as the planet earth. What Darwin did was to bring the human species into the ever-evolving cluster of earthly species. What our new knowledge of the evolution of human culture has done is to teach us that the religious dimension of human culture is as humanly created as the culture itself. For some time we have been ready to concede that religions other than our own are of human origin. We have found it more difficult to accept that even Christianity has been humanly created.

In a seminal book *The Meaning and End of Religion* (1963), the distinguished scholar of world religions W. Cantwell Smith proposed that we should stop using the word "religion" because it has now become ambiguous and misleading. He suggested we should replace it with two other terms: the "cumulative tradition" and "faith."

The term "faith" refers to the internal attitude of trust in relation to life. Christians have no monopoly of it, even though it has been one of their basic terms. Faith of some kind is essential to human existence. We humans cannot live well or long without faith. The absence of faith leads to depression, lack of motivation and despair. When Jesus said to the woman, "Your faith has made you whole," he was not referring to her beliefs but to her trust and attitude toward life. As a result of Smith's insight, the many and various religious traditions are today often referred to as "paths of faith."

Smith's term "cumulative tradition" refers to all the objective products of faith that have come to give character and identity to each path of faith. Such products are myths and stories, Holy Scriptures, creeds, dogmas, temples, social institutions, and sacred practices. The cumulative tradition marks out the path of faith being trodden in a particular culture. It is called cumulative because it keeps growing. It is the product of faith and not to be confused with faith. Although knowledge of the cumulative tradition serves to nurture the faith of later generations, it should never become the object of faith, for that would be idolatry. In a vibrant culture the inner experience of faith is continually manifesting itself in new creations as it responds to the circumstances of its time. As Smith said, "One's beliefs belong to the century one lives in, but what endures from generation to generation is the inner experience of faith."

A NEW CONTEXT FOR FAITH

It is in the context of the evolution of human culture that we must seek to understand the current crisis in the Christian path of faith. The expression of faith is undergoing radical change today because of the new way we look at the world in which we live. It is analogous to the way in which we no longer see the earth as the center and major part of the universe, but rather as a tiny planet in an almost infinite space-time universe of stars and nebulae. In the same way we find that the Christian path of faith is only one within a complex history of many diverse paths trodden by humans. Viewed from within the Christian cumulative tradition it appeared to consist of fixed and unchangeable truths revealed by God. But within the much wider context in which we must now study it, we find it to consist of products created by humans as they walked the Christian path of faith.

Furthermore, the Christian cumulative tradition has been evolving since the days of the patriarchs nearly four thousand years ago, and has been known by different names at different times in its history. The term "Christianity" by which it is known by most today did not come into use until the sixteenth century. Before that it was long known simply as "the faith," "Christian faith," or "Christian religion," which meant "the Christian mode of devotion." The very earliest name for it was simply "The Way." Perhaps that is still one of the best, being so like "path of faith."

During its four-thousand-year history, innumerable additions and omissions have taken place in the evolving Judeo-Christian cumulative tradition. But there has also been continuity. Moses, Jeremiah, Jesus, Paul, Augustine, Aquinas, Luther, down to Dietrich Bonhoeffer and Martin Luther King Jr. were all part of this evolving tradition. They all walked within this path of faith, yet their beliefs varied considerably since these reflected the different times in which they lived.

TWO AXIAL PERIODS

During this long cultural evolution, however, there have been two major periods of quite radical cultural change. The first of these is now often called the Axial Period. Our new awareness of this makes it necessary for us to re-think our division of earthly time. Christians have long used the supposed birth year of Jesus to order the calendar. That event was thought to cut history into two eras— BC and AD (hereafter, in keeping with their scholarly designations, BCE and CE). But this practice simply illustrates how Christians somewhat chauvinistically put their own stamp on the calendar.

Once we look at the totality of human cultures we find that the year 500 BCE marks the approximate center of a time of radical cultural change now labeled the Axial Period, or, to distinguish it from a later one, the First Axial Period. The term "Axial" was chosen because it seemed as if the evolution of human cultures was taking a giant turn on its axis and moving in another direction. This change occurred in a number of places in Asia, more or less simultaneously—at least relative to the hundred thousand years of evolving cultures that had preceded it.

For the first time in known human history, many great cultural traditions came under critical examination by insightful and courageous thinkers. These are known today as the prophets of Israel; in Iran the prophet Zoroaster; in India the Buddha, Mahavira, and Hindu seers; in China the teachers Confucius and Lao Tzu;

and in Greece the philosophers. As a result of their critical and creative reflections there emerged a new order of cultural traditions, different from the purely ethnic traditions that had preceded them. In the Far East the chief ones were Buddhism, Jainism, Hinduism, Confucianism, and Taoism. In the Middle East they were Zoroastrianism, Judaism, Platonism, and Stoicism. Within a few centuries Christianity and Islam evolved out of Judaism, and all three monotheistic traditions were strongly influenced by the Greek philosophers. These new post-Axial traditions replaced or absorbed the primal traditions that had preceded them—traditions that had been based both on ethnic ties and the veneration of the forces of nature. A number of good examples of these primal cultures are to be found in indigenous cultures not touched by the First Axial Period until modern times. Thus it was in the First Axial Period that the Judeo-Christian tradition came to birth.

The term "Second Axial Age" refers to the cultural and religious change by which the Christian West gave birth to the modern global, secular, and humanistic culture that is now spreading around the world. This secular culture emerged out of the Judeo-Christian tradition, just as the First Axial Age arose out of the ethnic and nature cultures that had preceded it. It is not Christian in the way Christendom was, but neither is it anti-Christian. It is best described as post-Christian, for it still reflects the values and customs of the tradition that gave it birth. Just what these values are we shall discuss in a later chapter.

CONTINUITY AND DISCONTINUITY

At this point I wish to show that at each of the two Axial Periods there has been both continuity and discontinuity. The old and the new exist in tension alongside each other for quite some time, often giving rise to bitter antagonism. During the transition the discontinuity is so sharply felt that the continuity becomes apparent only when viewed from a distance. That is why, living as we do within the Second Axial Period, we are so aware of the conflict between traditional Christendom and the secular world that we easily fail to see the continuity. On the other hand, we often fail to see the discontinuity that occurred at the First Axial Period because the Bible, by starting with creation, appears to be affirming the continuity.

Prior to the First Axial Period all human cultures explained the phenomena of nature as acts performed by a plethora of gods and spirits. In the early evolution of these cultures the gods were created by the symbol-making capacity of the human imagination. Each god had his or her own proper name and was allotted a particular function to perform. The word "god" was a generic term referring to a class of spiritual beings.

Then came the First Axial Period. In the sixth century BCE the Greek philosopher Xenophanes subjected the gods to critical examination. He condemned them for their immorality and poked fun at their anthropomorphic character. In India the Buddha took a different approach. He judged the gods to be irrelevant to the religious quest for human fulfillment; the gods were marginalized, and eventually faded from Buddhist terminology.

The Israelite prophets who pioneered the Judeo-Christian tradition first of all openly attacked the gods of the other nations, warning their own people not "to go after other gods to their own hurt." In the sixth century BCE they went much further, and, like Xenophanes, they also poked fun at the gods, scornfully dismissing them as having no reality; the gods were simply the creations of human imagination. Here was radical discontinuity with the past.

But unlike the Buddhists the Israelites retained the Hebrew word for "the gods" in its plural form—*elohim.* Here was continuity. Yet the word received a new meaning. The word that once denoted a class of beings now came to be used as a singular noun and soon came to be treated as a personal name, indeed as a replacement for the name of their earlier tribal God, Yahweh. For the Jews, henceforth, all divine power was believed to be concentrated in one unseeable spiritual force. Thus was born monotheism.

A further discontinuity has often been overlooked. Before the Babylonian Exile the people of Israel, like all other peoples, had a land of their own, and their gods had their own earthly dwelling-places, called temples. It was during and after the Exile that the

Jewish people ceased to be united by a dynasty and the possession of their own land. They became a community held together only by their faith in their cultural tradition. Soon they had to learn to do without a Temple and they replaced it with an entirely new kind of religious institution—the synagogue. Compared with the priestly-controlled temple, the synagogue can be called a lay institute; it existed for fellowship, prayer and the celebration of their tradition. It was in the Exile, during the First Axial Period, that what we today call Judaism—the Jewish path of faith—came to birth. In the process of this birth, a radical religious transition took place, one that can be summarized this way:

1. The pre-Axial gods were rejected and replaced by one God, conceived as an unseeable spiritual force that had created the universe and still controls human history.
2. The temple and its priesthood began to be replaced by the synagogue, Holy Scriptures, and lay-leadership, a process that was not completed until the final destruction of the Temple in 70 CE.

These same radical reforms continued into the two derivative paths of faith—Christian and Islamic. All three were monotheistic, all three had their respective Holy Scriptures, and the non-priestly institution of the synagogue became the prototype of both church and mosque. Unfortunately, as the three separate cumulative traditions subsequently developed their own elaborate complexities, Jew, Christian, and Muslim often lost sight of what all three had in common, including the radical nature of the religious transition that had taken place in the Axial Period.

THE SECULAR UNIVERSE

Let us now compare these radical changes of the First Axial Period with those taking place during the Second Axial Period. A key fact is that over the last five hundred years our understanding of origins has been turned upside down. Instead of believing ourselves to have been made in the image of a divine being, we find we are earthly organisms who have evolved biologically on this planet and then proceeded to create our cultures. And, like all other planetary organisms, we live a finite existence between conception and death. Compared with the time span of the earth, and even with the life of any particular species, the life of individual persons seems infinitesimally short. All this and more is what we mean when we speak of the modern world-view as secular or "this-worldly."

In this secular view of the universe, God, along with his heavenly dwelling-place, has lost objective reality. There is no need to postulate a supernatural creator to explain natural phenomena. Neither do we now expect divine providence to deliver us from our misfortunes. That is why, as theologian John Macquarrie observed, "among educated people throughout the world, the traditional kind of God-talk has virtually ceased." Here lies the discontinuity. We humans used to see ourselves as the creation of a supernatural deity; now we find it is we who, by creating language, also created such important concepts as God. We can even write a history of God, that is, a history of what the term has meant, as Karen Armstrong has done so brilliantly.

At the time of the First Axial Period the gods were declared to be unreal, being the products of human imagination. In the Second Axial Period the God of classical monotheism has increasingly lost reality as a divine personal being and has widely come to be seen as a humanly created symbol, referring to a cluster of supreme values. The Second Axial Period has introduced such major discontinuity with the Christian past that the majority of Christians and non-Christians alike fail to see any real connection between the modern secular world and the Christian world out of which it emerged.

That is why the Judeo-Christian tradition is at the crossroads. Western culture has become polarized. At one extreme Christian fundamentalists flatly reject all modern thinking that conflicts with the Christian doctrines they loyally but myopically defend. Fundamentalists, both Christian and Muslim, treat the coming of the humanistic and secular world as the spread of the domain of Satan and hence an enemy to fought. Even the main line churches, now struggling to retain their identity, too often fall into the same superficial judgment about the origin and nature of the secular world.

Yet between about 1880 and 1950 Christian thinkers made a valiant attempt to accommodate the traditional Christian path to the challenges of the modern secular world. They were known as the Catholic Modernists and the Protestant Liberals. While Catholic Modernism was quickly crushed, Protestant Liberalism flourished for a time. It is now declining within the mainline churches with the result that they are tending to become more conservative and traditional.

At the other extreme of the polarized Western world is the growing number of people who conclude that Christianity is now a spent force, a superstitious survival from the past. (I define superstition as any belief or practice that has outlived the now obsolete cultural context in which it was appropriate.) Secularists are those who abandon all association with the Christian past.

Yet the modern secular world originated in the Christian West. That is an undeniable fact. For this reason the secular world stands in a unique relation with the Judeo-Christian tradition, even though it is increasingly in conflict with much of the content of the Christian cumulative tradition. Certainly the secular world is far from perfect. But neither was the receding Christendom perfect, marked as it was by such things as the Inquisition, the burning of witches, and its patriarchal power structure, to name but a few of its deficiencies. So the modern world does not have to be perfect before we can acknowledge it to be a product of the Christendom. But the question remains whether we have carelessly and foolishly stumbled into a blind path or find ourselves entering a genuine new stage in the evolution of the Judeo-Christian tradition. Too little attention has been given to this question by Christian and non-Christian alike.

Christians who reject the modern secular world, be they fundamentalist, conservative, or traditionalist, may be impeding the legitimate evolution of the very tradition they wish so desperately to defend. On the other hand, secularists who reject Christianity entirely and refuse to acknowledge indebtedness to the cultural matrix out of which the modern world has emerged are cutting themselves off from their cultural and spiritual roots. As plants without roots wither and die, so cultures that forget their past do the same.

FACING THE DILEMMA

This is the dilemma we face at the crossroads that Christianity has reached. That is why in the last two decades an increasing number of as yet small groups of concerned people have arisen around the world. They wish to acknowledge the legitimacy of the modern secular world but at the same time stress the values it has inherited from the past and may be in danger of losing. Such Groups include the Sea of Faith Network now operating in the UK and New Zealand and Australia, the Snowstar Institute of Canada, and the Center for Progressive Christianity in the USA, to name but a few.

Another of these is the Westar Institute. It is a unique kind of academic institution founded in 1985 by an American New Testament scholar, Dr. Robert Funk. He came to recognize that scholars of religion were not wholly free in their pursuit of truth; those in seminaries were constrained by church pressure and those in universities by issues of academic advancement. So he invited all qualified scholars interested in the unimpeded study of Christian origins to join with him in the activities of the Westar Institute, based in Santa Rosa, California. Some 200 scholars have participated in the project, though not more than about 75 at any one time. They meet twice a year for three days to discuss the papers they have prepared on chosen or assigned topics.

Known as the Fellows of the Institute, these scholars do not confine themselves to the Bible, but view all relevant extant material from the past. They study it objectively, as open-minded historians, rather than as people seeking to confirm already-held religious convictions. In addition to the scholars are some three thousand associate members who support the work financially and who are free to attend the scholarly meetings and listen to the debates. This is the first academic institution in which biblical study has been carried out by a community of scholars, in an atmosphere of complete freedom, and within the hearing of the public. Guided solely by the criteria of honesty and integrity, they use a simple method of voting to arrive at a scholarly consensus after vigorously debating the issues.

The Institute believes the churches can best respond positively to the crisis Christianity now faces by helping lay people to become biblically and theologically literate. In March of this year [2004] the Westar Institute held its spring meeting in New York, discussing "The Future of the Judeo-Christian Tradition in the Second Axial Period." I was privileged to be among the four speakers from UK and the six from USA who were invited to deliver lectures; some sections of my lecture have been incorporated in this book.

In the next chapter I shall discuss what the Westar Institute has found out about the original Jesus of Nazareth. What has long been hidden from view behind the church portrait of the Christ figure throws considerable light on where the Christian path of faith is now going.

3

EXCAVATING JESUS

U p until two hundred years ago it was assumed without question in the Christian world that Jesus was no ordinary human but a divine figure. The Bible seemed to make this abundantly clear, for it was further assumed that the gospel records provide us with a completely reliable account of what Jesus said and did. Not only do Christian fundamentalists believe that to this day, but so do most traditional Christians. Yet these assumptions have been seriously undermined by the revolution that has taken place in biblical study in the last two centuries. New Testament scholars today widely agree that none of the gospel writers were eyewitnesses of the events they narrated, for they were writing between forty and seventy years after Jesus had died. At that time the oral stories about him were not only still in a fluid state, but were being rapidly embellished and even added to by creative and devout imagination.

The gospel writers were not historians in our sense of the word. They were primarily preachers; that is why their works are called gospels, or proclamations of Good News. The writer of the Fourth Gospel must not be accused of falsifying the evidence when he created the speeches he put into the mouth of Jesus. That had been common practice since Herodotus (c. 485–425 BCE). Indeed, the writer of the Fourth Gospel tells his readers at the end that he has written as he did for the express purpose of leading them to believe that Jesus is the Christ, the Son of God. He was doing no more than what preachers and Sunday School teachers do to this day when they use their imagination to fill out a biblical story. There is no great harm in this practice. The problem arises only when what has been said in that manner is appealed to as historical evidence.

FROM STRAUSS TO SCHWEITZER

The biblical revolution was set in motion by David Strauss as long ago as 1835 with his epoch-making book, *The Life of Jesus Critically Examined.* In 1966 the scholarly Bishop Stephen Neill referred to this book as a "turning point in the history of the Christian faith." Unfortunately, most people in the churches failed to notice.

Although Strauss tended to go to extremes, he nevertheless showed convincingly how, during the period of fluid oral tradition, the early Christians both reshaped and invented the stories they told about Jesus. To fill in missing details, they often turned back to their Bible—the Hebrew Scriptures. We are told several times how they "searched the scriptures" to understand what had happened. That is why there are such close parallels between the story of the crucifixion and Psalm 22, between the transfiguration of Jesus on the high mountain and the shining face of Moses on Mt. Sinai, between the ascension of Jesus into heaven and the ascension of Elijah.

Strauss was the first to draw attention to the myth-making capacity of the human imagination, a faculty of which we have now become much more aware. Thus the figure of Jesus Christ portrayed by the gospels must now be distinguished from the original Jesus. What eventually became the traditional portrait of the divine Christ, as expressed in Christian dogma and worshipped by the church, is largely the creation of the early church. In 1865 Strauss wrote *The Christ of Faith and the Jesus of History.* By the "Jesus of History" he meant the original historical figure. By the "Christ of Faith" (or "Christ of Dogma," as some now prefer) he meant the figure created by the myth-making faculty of the early Christians. Thus it was not Jesus but the "Christ of Faith" who claimed to be the Son of God, and who said "I am the Way, the Truth and the Life. No man comes unto the Father except by me." It has been necessary to make that distinction ever since. It is reflected in such books as *Jesus the Man and the Myth* (James P. Mackey, 1979), and *Jesus Who Became the Christ* (Peter De Rosa, 1975).

The work of Strauss prompted scholars to search for the historical Jesus, and during the nineteenth century many "lives of Jesus" were written. But their selection and interpretation of the material was often very subjective. The "Jesus" they claimed to have recovered was the kind of figure they wanted to find there. As one Catholic critic put it, "In searching for the historical Jesus the modern scholars have looked down a deep well and what they saw was the reflection of their own Protestant liberal face."

The search came almost to an abrupt end in 1906 with the publication of Albert Schweitzer's epoch-making book, *The Quest of the Historical Jesus.* Schweitzer showed the inadequacy of all the attempts to date to write the life of Jesus. Then he largely adopted the position of Johannes Weiss, who in 1893 had written *Jesus' Preaching of the Kingdom of God.* There Weiss concluded that the chief mission of Jesus was to proclaim the imminent end of the world and the arrival of a transcendental Kingdom—a proclamation that turned out to be false. Schweitzer describes this in very moving words:

> Jesus, in the knowledge that he is the coming Son of Man, lays hold of the wheel of the world to set it moving on that last revolution which is to bring all ordinary history to a close. It refuses to turn, and he throws himself upon it. Then it does turn and it crushes him. Instead of bringing in the eschatological conditions, he has destroyed them.

As Schweitzer saw it, Jesus died on the cross a disillusioned man, and that is why he cried out, "My God, why have you forsaken me?" Schweitzer said that the original Jesus was wholly a man of his own time, and not necessarily one we would be attracted to. He even ventured to say that any historical knowledge of Jesus we do uncover might even offend us. Schweitzer concluded that we must be content to let Jesus stay in his own place and time. What remained important for Schweitzer was what he called "the mighty spiritual force which streams forth from him," and he declared that to be "the foundation of Christianity."

The next fifty years saw relatively few attempts to write "a life of Jesus." Most scholars accepted that Jesus was an eschatological figure who spoke in terms of apocalyptic imagery that we today find quite bizarre. Rudolf Bultmann, the most radical New Testament scholar of the twentieth century, concluded that we know practically nothing about Jesus except that the Romans put him to death for reasons that are none too clear.

THE JESUS SEMINAR

In 1985 the Westar Institute began a new search to rediscover the original Jesus and it took a quite novel form. The scholars engaged in this task became known as "The Jesus Seminar." Their first task was to establish a database, and this was published in 1992 as *The Complete Gospels.* They then painstakingly sifted the data for all clues that could genuinely be regarded as pointing to the historical Jesus. Their work has now been published in two major volumes: *The Five Gospels: What Did Jesus Really Say?* (1993) and *The Acts of Jesus: What Did Jesus Really Do?* (1998). The work of the Jesus Seminar has been strongly condemned by fundamentalists and by traditionalist scholars, who often blame the group for undermining the traditional figure of the Christ, though in fact this had already been done by 150 years of scholarship. What is easily overlooked is that the Jesus Seminar has been more positive in its results than the radical New Testament scholarship of the previous fifty years.

The task of the biblical historian, like that of any modern historian, has been compared with that of the detective. As the detective tries to reconstruct the scene of the crime on the basis of surviving clues, the historian tries to reconstruct past events on the basis of extant written sources. Parallel to the role of historians is that of archaeologists; they try to reconstruct a mental picture of life in the past by sifting through the physical deposits left by the past.

In the search for the historical Jesus these two approaches have recently been combined in one book. One of the leading figures of the Jesus seminar, John Dominic Crossan, collaborated with Jonathan L. Reed, a New Testament archaeologist, in writing *Excavating Jesus: Beneath the Stones, Behind the Texts* (2002).

When archaeologists excavate, they find they must carefully uncover the past layer by layer in the reverse order of that in which it has accumulated. It is rather like that with the search for the historical Jesus. We start with a picture of Jesus in our minds, one that we have absorbed from a cultural background long shaped by Christian tradition. Taking a lead from the title of the book just mentioned, I now wish to take you on a journey backwards in time. We shall remove, layer by layer, the growing beliefs that gradually turned the man Jesus into the Christ figure worshipped in the churches. (The fact that I have arrived at 9 Layers is of no significance.)

A JOURNEY BACKWARD IN TIME

Let us start with the latest, Layer 9, which I call The Dogmatic Layer. In 381 CE the Second Ecumenical Council referred to Jesus as "the only begotten Son of God, Very God of very God, by whom all things were made, who came down from heaven and was made man." These words became a permanent part of the Nicene Creed, and some of them are familiar to us because they appear in the second verse of the popular Christmas carol "O Come All Ye Faithful."

Layer 9 clearly draws from Layer 8, found in the Fourth Gospel. About 100 CE the author of John began, "In the beginning was the Word, and the Word was with God, and the Word was God. All things were made through him. In him was life . . . And the Word became flesh and dwelt among us." It was a quite new and daring thought at the time to trace the story of Jesus back to the beginning of time. We know that when this gospel first appeared it surprised and even alarmed some Christians. It did not win full acceptance in the church until near the end of the second century; but thereafter it became the favorite gospel of many. It is only in these top two layers that Jesus Christ is assigned a pre-history as the divine Son of God. We are told it was he who created the world and who, only much later, became incarnate in the historical figure known as Jesus. Note that these two late layers assert that God became man. But in the earlier layers we now turn to, it was the other way round: Jesus became the Christ, the Son of God. In other words, a man became God.

A clue to Layer 7 is found in the genealogy compiled by Luke. After narrating birth stories about Jesus, it traces the human ancestry of Jesus back through the generations from his father Joseph to Seth, the Son of Adam, the Son of God. As a Gentile Christian,

Luke set out to show that Jesus was a true representative of all humankind, Gentiles as well as Jews.

This had the effect of widening the more limited genealogy provided by the Jewish Christian who wrote Matthew. He had been content to show that Jesus was a true Jew, and therefore traced his ancestry back only as far as Abraham. We may call this Layer 6. In layers 7 and 6 the evangelists were assuming the humanity of Jesus but, by means of the birth stories they each supplied, they were implying that the birth of Jesus was part of a divine plan by which Jesus was destined to become the Son of God and Savior of the world.

But how was the man Jesus to become divine? We have some surviving hints of the process by which this took place. What we may call Layer 5 is found in Mark, the earliest gospel. Mark provides neither birth story nor genealogy, but starts with the story of Jesus' baptism, in which we are told that "The spirit descended on Jesus like a dove and a voice came from heaven, 'You are my beloved son; with you I am well pleased'." Thus for Mark's gospel, it was at his baptism that the man Jesus was chosen and ordained by God to be divine.

This story gave rise in early Christian thought to the "adoption" theory of how Jesus became divine. This doctrine was eventually declared heretical because it was in conflict with later developments, especially layers 8–9.

But Mark records another story from early tradition by which he suggests that it was only during the teaching mission of Jesus that people began to regard Jesus as more than an ordinary man. We may call this Layer 4. In telling the story of the disciples with Jesus at Caesarea Philippi, Mark puts into the mouth of Peter the confession "You are the Messiah"; but he adds a strange twist, for he says Jesus immediately charged the disciples to tell no one about him. Scholars now refer to this odd comment in Mark as the Messianic Secret. It is regarded as a Markan literary device used to explain why there was no public talk of Jesus' Messiahship during his lifetime, a "missing link" that Mark seems to have been aware of.

It has been commonly theorized that Mark was not a Palestinian Jew, probably not even a Christian Jew, but a Christian Gentile who may have been writing in Rome. This would explain why he has the Roman centurion who attended the crucifixion of Jesus say, "Truly the man was a Son of God"—thereby hinting that it was the way Jesus died, his bearing on the cross, that first alerted people to his divine nature—and that therefore Gentiles were just as likely to recognize the truth as the Jews, and perhaps even more so. This we may call Layer 3.

As we have been uncovering these layers, we see that the point at which Jesus was being affirmed as divine is becoming later and later in time. One more layer remains. The author of Acts seems to have preserved an early tradition that the first recognition of Jesus as Messiah and Son of God actually arose after his death, and that it was associated with the rise of the Easter faith. For in Acts we hear Peter say, "Let all the house of Israel know that this Jesus whom you crucified, God has made both Lord and Christ." This is Layer 2.

Layers 7–2 have survived in the Synoptic Gospels, written between 70 and 90 CE, and Acts, which some scholars now date to about 115 CE. All these texts were written in Greek and reflect the Christian beliefs current in the Greek-speaking Gentile churches founded by Paul. Paul's own writings come from about 48–55 CE and the influence of his beliefs is undoubtedly present in the synoptic gospels, though he agrees with the author of Acts that Jesus' divine sonship was revealed by his resurrection.

In fact, so strong was the influence of Paul that some now claim he was the real founder of Christianity. He was certainly the founder of the Gentile stream of Christianity, and it was this that eventually triumphed. This brings us to the strangest fact of all. The man who has had most influence in shaping Christianity and in determining the framework of all Christian dogma never met the historical Jesus.

To be sure, some years after his conversion, Paul went twice to Jerusalem to meet the disciples who had known the historical Jesus. But in referring to these meetings in his letter to the Galatians, he made no mention of anything he learned about Jesus. Further, on his own admission he was not interested in information about the historical Jesus.

If we are to reach back to the original Jesus we must remove the very strong influence of Paul, Layer 1, and go to those earliest Christians at Jerusalem who included the original disciples and also James, the blood brother of Jesus. About these first Christians, commonly known today as the "Jewish Christians," we know very little except that when the Romans destroyed Jerusalem in 70 CE, those who were still alive escaped to Pella in Jordan. They were ignored by the Gentile church and after some centuries died out without a trace.

FOOTPRINTS OF JESUS

Have we now come to rock bottom and found nothing? No, for here the work of the Jesus Seminar has produced some interesting and unexpected results. It now seems likely that the four canonical gospels were not the earliest. They were preceded by two others, now known as Q and the Gospel of Thomas. We have known about Q for some time because as nineteenth century scholars came to be aware, it had been incorporated into both Matthew and Luke; but we did not recognize its full significance until the discovery in 1945 of the Gospel of Thomas. Fellows of the Jesus Seminar have written excellent books about these, including *The Lost Gospel—Q* by Burton L. Mack and *The Fifth Gospel* by Stephen Patterson.

What is most surprising about these two apparently early gospels is that they say little or nothing about the life, death, and resurrection of Jesus, but are almost exclusively concerned with what Jesus said. This suggests that after his death, the chief focus of his followers was not on his life but on his teaching. Hence the scholars of the Jesus Seminar have concluded that Jesus of Nazareth was primarily a teacher of wisdom, a sage. It was only some time after his death, and chiefly under the influence of Paul, that the initial emphasis on Jesus as a teacher was displaced by increasing interest in Jesus as the crucified Messiah, the Lord, and the divine Son of God.

On the basis of the work of the Jesus Seminar in general, and on the study of these two earliest gospels in particular, we arrive as close as we possibly can to the original Jesus. And what do we learn?

First let us posit several important negatives:

- He never claimed to be the Son of God.
- He never claimed to be the Messiah.
- He was not an apocalyptic prophet, announcing the imminent end of the world.
- He was not the founder of Christianity.
- He was not a Christian.

WHAT CAN WE SAY POSITIVELY ABOUT JESUS?

The person we now call Jesus of Nazareth was a Galilean Jew who lived between the death of Herod the Great in 4 BCE and the end of Pilate's governorship of Palestine in 36 CE. He was born and brought up in Nazareth, although later tradition shifted his birthplace to Bethlehem in order to bring it into line with a supposed ancient prophecy. The trip to Bethlehem, the three wise men, the flight to Egypt, the shepherds in the fields, and the kinship with John the Baptist are all Christian fictions from the late first century. The Galilee in which Jesus lived out his life was not highly regarded by the Jerusalem Jews. They judged it to be semi-pagan, because of its mixed blood and foreign influence. Nazareth was a Galilean village only four miles from the thriving Greco-Roman city of Sepphoris (which the New Testament strangely never mentions).

The mother of Jesus was called Mary and the name of his putative father was probably Joseph. He had sisters and brothers, one of whom, James, later became the leader of the Jerusalem Christians. The account of his virginal birth was a fictional story that arose later to satisfy growing theological insistence on his divinity.

It is highly probable that Jesus was baptized by John the Baptist and became one of his followers for a time. Then he launched his own career in Galilee and some of John's followers left John to become disciples of Jesus. Jesus became an itinerant sage, wandering from place to place, teaching, healing and living on handouts. His native language was the dialect of Aramaic current in Galilee, a few words of which, like *talitha cumi*, have survived in the gospel material.

Since he was brought up so close to the Greco-Roman city Sepphoris, it is likely that Greek was his second language. If so, little or nothing of what he said in Greek has come down to us, even though Greek was the language in which the Christian tradition took shape. We do not know for certain whether he could read and write, but being reared as a Jew he probably could. We need to remember that he was brought up in a pre-literate society, where only a small minority were good readers and fewer still ever wrote—a fact that is reflected in the term "scribe," the job description of those who earned their living by reading and writing for those who could not.

His chief followers were Peter, James, and John, and this band included some women. The number twelve is probably a tradition added later as Christians began to interpret their movement as the New Israel and recalled that the old Israel had consisted of 12 tribes.

In his lifetime Jesus gained a reputation as a healer. He usually healed by the use of words, and from today's perspective his success may have been in the area of psychosomatic cures. But by no means do all of the healings attributed to Jesus in the gospels have an historical core. Of course, Jesus, being a man of his time, fully accepted the current beliefs of his day about the power of evil spirits and in this respect he almost certainly practiced exorcism. But he did not perform such miracles as stilling a storm, walking on water, feeding 5000 people with a few loaves of bread and a couple of fish, and turning water into wine. Indeed even Mark records that when people asked Jesus for some heavenly sign to demonstrate the coming of the Kingdom, he refused their request.

Jesus became famous for his teaching and crowds came to hear him. This made him very popular with many people, but apparently he was not well received in his hometown. Further, he met with opposition from religious authorities, though in fact much of the enmity narrated in the gospels reflects later conflicts between Christians and Jews.

We do not know how long his teaching and healing career lasted. The gospels imply a relatively short period of one to three years. When Jesus went up to Jerusalem for the last time he was not aware that it would be his last. He may have ridden into the city on an ass as a symbolic act, but not as a way of asserting his Messiahship. The story of the dramatic "cleansing" of the Temple originated with some historical act by which he challenged the Temple authorities. This may have been what led to his arrest, after which he was charged by the High Priest and handed over to the Romans, who executed him. It is almost certain that his followers fled when he was arrested, and that the accounts of the trials and Peter's denial are fictional. The burial of Jesus is another fictional narrative carried out by a fictional character, Joseph of Arimathea. The stories of the empty tomb are likewise all fictional.

Our search for the original Jesus leaves us with only his voiceprints and his footprints. The voiceprints we shall look at in the next chapter. The footprints are far from being those of an otherworldly, divine figure who performed all sorts of miracles. Rather they point to a person who was very human and "this-worldly." He enjoyed life. He liked his food and wine to the extent of being called a glutton and a winebibber by his enemies. He cared for people. He mixed with undesirables. He incurred the wrath of the religious people of his day by stepping outside the boundaries of what was regarded as respectable Jewish behavior. He had a great sense of humor. Though this faint outline deeply disappoints those looking for a divine figure, the historical Jesus seems to have been the sort of person to whom modern secular people can relate much more readily than they can to the traditional otherworldly Christ figure. Indeed, the latter belongs to a mythical world now altogether foreign to us.

CRUCIFIXION AND RESURRECTION

But if Jesus was not a divine miracle-worker from another world, what was there about this wholly human person that made his followers remember him and eventually, in their devotion, turn him into the divine Christ? Why was it that Christianity burst into life some time shortly after his death? These are not easy questions to answer at this distance in time.

We too easily forget that even on the basis of the New Testament testimony, Jesus seems to have been something of an enigma in his own lifetime. Certainly there was something striking and unusual about him. But that led some to regard him as mad. It led others to see him as a public nuisance who had to be got out of the way. Only a small number were permanently attracted to him—but for what reason?

Paul of Tarsus, who largely shaped Christianity, was himself attracted to Jesus because of a spiritual experience he had while traveling to Damascus, but that occurred after the life of Jesus was over. The event within the life of Jesus that chiefly interested Paul was his crucifixion. He wrote to the Corinthians, "I decided to know nothing among you except Jesus Christ and him crucified." If it had not done so before, the crucifixion became the focal point of Christianity thereafter. A quarter of each of the gospels is devoted to it. It dominated medieval Christian thought and practice through the Middle Ages, as demonstrated by the devotional prevalence of the crucifix. Its most recent resurgence appears in the interest shown by conservative Christians, Catholic and Protestant alike, in Mel Gibson's film *The Passion of the Christ.*

Yet there was nothing unique about the crucifixion, as such. There were thousands of crucifixions in those days, and many were carried out by Jews themselves. It must have been something else for which Jesus was initially remembered.

During the nineteenth and early twentieth centuries defenders of traditional Christianity fastened on the resurrection of Jesus as the key. This was treated as a unique and extraordinary miracle by which a man had overcome death and returned to a new and glorified life. It was frequently claimed that this miracle sparked off the rise of Christianity. Much was made of what was still assumed to be historical evidence for this. Only slowly, roughly between about 1920–1950, was it gradually conceded by scholars that the so-called historical evidence belonged to the realm of devout myth rather than history.

We must also allow for the fact that, as Schweitzer wisely conceded, what attracted people in the first century is not necessarily what we of the twenty-first century would find attractive. We are in a very different cultural situation from that of Jesus, and also from that of those who shaped Christianity. But if the attraction was something that could also appeal to us, it must have been associated with his humanity.

I observed earlier that one of the discoveries of the Jesus Seminar is that the two earliest gospels, Q and Thomas, made no reference to either the crucifixion or resurrection of Jesus. They were chiefly concerned to record his teaching. This makes it appear that the teaching of Jesus was what triggered the initial growth of Christianity. Once again defenders of traditional Christianity argue that this could not explain why Jesus was crucified. To this we can justifiably reply, "And why not? Socrates was put to death for his teaching. And through the ages the church itself put numerous people to death just because of their teaching, burning at the stake all those judged to be teaching heresy." Jesus was crucified, not because of any miracles, but because of what he taught.

4

THE RECOVERY OF JESUS' TEACHING

The Fellows of the Westar Institute spent nearly fifteen years searching the ancient records for evidence depicting the historical Jesus of Nazareth. They removed the mantle of the heavenly Christ figure under which the early church had long hidden the original human Jesus, and they uncovered the latter's footprints and voiceprints. Then they devoted their autumn meeting in 1999 to the theme of "The Once and Future Jesus." They began to explore what the original Jesus could mean for the modern world. For this task they would use the already assembled database of what Jesus really said and did.

Let me first sketch the teachings of the Jesus they discovered. We find they fall into two categories—short aphorisms (or one-liners) and parables. Now these are exactly the same genres we find in the Jewish sages of the Israelite Wisdom tradition. That in itself is quite a discovery, for if Jesus spoke chiefly in aphorisms and parables as the sages did, then he was closer to the Israelite sages than to the Israelite prophets.

To appreciate this we must recall that the Israelite sages represented one of four main streams of thought in the Old Testament— the Priestly, the Prophetic, the Royalist, and the Wisdom traditions. The Priestly tradition (found in the Torah or Books of Moses) became the basis of Judaism. The Royalist tradition (found chiefly in Samuel and Kings but reflected elsewhere) provided the basis of Christianity, which claimed Jesus to be the promised Messianic King. The Prophetic Tradition (chiefly in the books of the prophets) was later revived by Muhammad and became the basis of Islam.

SAGES FOCUS ON EVERYDAY LIFE

But the Wisdom tradition was largely neglected by Jew, Christian, and Muslim alike. It is found in the books of Proverbs, Job, Ecclesiastes, some Psalms, the Wisdom of Solomon, and Ecclesiasticus. And when we look exclusively at the Wisdom tradition we find a strange thing. The sages, unlike the prophets and priests, showed little

51

interest in the Exodus Tradition, the Davidic Dynasty, or the historical destiny of the Israelite people. They focused on the issues of everyday life, as experienced by all humankind.

Modern scholars have called the Israelite sages the Hebrew humanists. They were not concerned with religion as that term is commonly understood today. They were interested in how to deal with life's problems and frustrations. They did occasionally refer to "God" or "the Lord," and even spoke of reverence for God as the beginning of Wisdom. But they introduced the divine name as if it referred to the cosmic order of the natural world. (We need to remember that Hebrew had no word equivalent to our "nature.") For the sages, "God" symbolized the way the world operates. For them, reverence for God meant reverence for nature—that is, learning to accept the way the world works and responding to it appropriately.

Once we remove from the gospels the sayings that the gospel writers created and put into the mouth of Jesus, we find that like the sages before him, Jesus did not say much about religion. Indeed, his mode of discourse was what we today call secular, meaning "this-worldly." He talked about daily life, the need to care for one another, and the problems that bring divisiveness and hurt in personal relationships. He made frequent reference to daily scenes and events such as vineyards, fields, shepherding, building, the hiring of workers, the lending of money, and the like.

Also like the sages before him, when Jesus referred to God, he was talking chiefly about what we call nature. The writer of Ecclesiasticus said, "Good things and bad, life and death, poverty and wealth all come from the Lord." Similarly Jesus said, "God causes the sun to rise on the bad and the good, and sends rain on the just and the unjust." But Jesus saw nature as a fatherly figure, much as we speak of nature as mother. Jesus was identifying the Heavenly Father with what we call Nature when he said, "Take a look at the birds of the sky: they don't plant or harvest, or gather into barns. Yet your heavenly Father feeds them. Notice how the wild lilies grow: they don't slave and they never spin. Yet let me tell you, even Solomon at the height of his glory was never decked out like one of them. If God dresses up the grass in the field, which is here today and tomorrow is thrown into the oven, won't God care for you even more?"

The Israelite sage closest to Jesus is Ecclesiastes, for both deal with issues common to all humans irrespective of their cultural differences. They were both concerned with the best way to find personal fulfillment in the face of all the enigmas that life presents. But in the quality and depth of his teaching Jesus far surpassed Ecclesiastes and the other sages who had preceded him. Jesus lifted the Wisdom stream to a new level in large part by transforming the parable into a unique new genre, a development for which he rightly became famous during his own lifetime.

FAITH, HOPE, RESPONSIBILITY

Jesus taught people to look into the future with faith and hope, but he never encouraged his listeners to let God take over their lives and make all their decisions for them, as do some evangelicals today. Rather, like the sages before him, he urged people to take full responsibility for their lives and to make every effort to make the right decision in every situation. That is why he told the story of the foolish man who built his house on the sand and the wise man who built his house on a rock. We should note that it was not because of divine providence that the one house stood firm while the other perished. It was due to the wisdom of the man who built on the rock.

Similarly Jesus urged, "Struggle to get in through the narrow door; I'm telling you, many will try to get in but won't be able." He encouraged people to take full responsibility for their actions and to work for the common good. This was lost sight of when, through the influence of Augustine, the later church placed a strong emphasis on faith (which entailed believing that Christ's death brought forgiveness). When the fifth-century Christian monk Pelagius tried to call his fellow-Christians back to the moral exhortations of Jesus, the church condemned his philosophy as heresy. If Jesus had been miraculously transplanted from first-century Palestine to the medieval world of Christendom, he could well have been burned at the stake as a heretic.

Being a Jew, Jesus was more concerned with how people acted than with what they believed. To this day the Jewish Way is known as orthopraxy (right action), in contrast with what became the Christian Way of orthodoxy (right belief). In urging people to right action, Jesus manifested a surprising measure of freedom in relation to the culture in which he was reared—and he encouraged others to do the same. Take for example what he said about sabbath observance, which is enjoined in Judaism's basic code, the Ten Commandments: "The sabbath day was created for Adam and Eve, not Adam and Eve for the sabbath day. So the son of Adam [that is, humankind] lords it over even the sabbath day." Similarly, Jesus did not feel bound by the Jewish dietary laws of his day. "Listen to me all of you, and try to understand! It's not what goes into a person from the outside that can defile; rather it's what comes out of the person that defiles." He advised people not to become imprisoned in the traditions of the past, observing that "Nobody pours young wine into old wineskins, otherwise the wine will burst the skins and destroy both the wine and the skins. Instead, young wine is for new wineskins."

In short, Jesus talked much more about how to live wisely and act righteously than he did about what to believe about God. That is why the well-known Sermon on the Mount—all of which comes from Q and thus reflects the earliest written memories of him—is so very different from what is put into the mouth of Jesus in the Gospel of John.

THE KINGDOM OF GOD

The chief theme running through the teaching of Jesus was not God but the kingdom of God. Jesus did not invent this term, for we find it occasionally in the earlier sages. Jesus fastened upon it, however, and made it central to his teaching. Perhaps he did so because many of his fellow Jews hoped for the restoration of the kingdom of David as the answer to the Roman occupation of their land. But the kingdom envisaged by Jesus was very different from both the Empire of Rome and the former kingdom of David.

In the ancient world the kingdom was the normal social institution that had evolved for the ordering of society. The king dispensed justice, and his royal authority prevented society from falling into disorder and chaos. But since even kings could become despots and dictators, Jesus used the term "kingdom of God" to refer to the ideal way of ordering human society.

Kings and emperors imposed their authority from above. But when Jesus spoke of the kingdom of God he was not referring to a power structure that would be imposed from above—not even by a supernatural God. Some early Christians, however, found this beyond their ability to understand. Adopting teachings attributed to John the Baptist, they put into the mouth of Jesus the apocalyptic description of the arrival of the kingdom as a sudden cataclysmic event. That is how Jesus, even by the time of Paul, was already being turned into an eschatological prophet who had come to announce the imminent end of the world.

But these apocalyptic warnings of a devastating end-time about to arrive are in conflict with what Jesus actually taught. He said the kingdom of God would come quietly and unobtrusively: "You won't be able to observe the coming of the kingdom of God. People are not going to be able to say, 'Look, here it is!' or 'Over there!' In actual fact, the kingdom of God is right there in your presence." In a similar vein Jesus likened the spread of the kingdom of God to leaven working its way quietly through a batch of dough. Unlike the kingdoms of the world, which impose authority from above, the kingdom of God would spread from the bottom, as people developed self-discipline and mutual concern for one another.

Many of the parables of Jesus start with the words, "The kingdom of God is like. . . ." Here we find Jesus talking about human attitudes toward life and the nature of human relationships. Jesus taught people to look into the future with faith and hope and not to get worked up and over-anxious: "Don't fret about life—what you're going to eat, or about your body—what you're going to wear.

Remember, there is more to living than food and clothing." In the kingdom of God people would get the best out of life, both for themselves and for others. Recognizing this, someone later put into his mouth the well-known line, "I have come that you may have life and have it more abundantly."

Jesus had a fine sense of humor. He used hyperbole to great effect and his pithy sayings were so striking that people remembered and retold them; yet, once they became recorded in Holy Scriptures, solemn readers of the Bible in later ages often missed the humor.

- It's easier for a camel to squeeze through the eye of a needle than for a rich man to get into the kingdom of God!
- Why do you notice the speck in your friend's eye, but overlook the log in your own?
- When someone wants to sue you for your coat, let that person have your tunic as well.

Howls of laughter would surely have greeted that remark, for since people in those days wore only two garments (an inner and an outer), such an action would have left the person naked.

By almost universal agreement, the most important injunction in the teaching of Jesus is brotherly love, the subject of perhaps his best-known parable—that of the Good Samaritan. Christians have long taught that the two most important commandments given by Jesus are these: "Love the Lord your God with all your heart and soul and mind and strength. And love your neighbor as yourself." But they too often forget that Jesus did not formulate these; as a good Jew, he was simply quoting from the Hebrew Bible, where these words are found, respectively, in Deuteronomy 6:5 and Leviticus 19:18.

Where Jesus was wholly original was in the now famous words, "Love your enemies." This was a revolutionary statement in his day and it still is. He expounded it further:

Tell me, if you love those who love you, why should you be commended for that? Even the despised toll collectors do as much, don't they? But I tell you—Don't react violently against one who is evil: when someone slaps you on the right cheek, turn the other as well. When anyone forces you to go for one mile, go an extra mile. Give to the one who begs from you; don't turn away the one who tries to borrow from you.

The injunction to love one's enemies is not only unique to the teaching of Jesus, but is so revolutionary that many have rejected it as absurd. In my own country, New Zealand, in 1942 a Christian pacifist was pleading his case before the tribunal. He explained that, as Christian, he was bound to love his enemies and therefore could not participate in military action. The magistrate poured scorn on him and said it was absurd to suggest that one could love Nazi Germans. Similarly, American Christians today think it is absurd to extend love to Saddam Hussein and Osama bin Laden.

The human Jesus, then, was a sage who taught some highly revolutionary things in describing the human behavior appropriate to the kingdom of God. His teaching caught people's attention and made its mark on their memories because it was so different from what they had heard before. "They were astonished at his teaching," wrote Mark, "since unlike the scholars he taught on his own authority."

While some of the aphorisms of Jesus were quite clear and direct in their challenge to the customs and mores of the day, some of what he said was intentionally puzzling. People were left to work out the implications for themselves. Even his parables sometimes had an unexpected sting in the tail. Jesus did not set out to replace the Ten Commandments with a set of new directives. He encouraged people to work out for themselves what was the right action to take and to do so on the basis of a few basic principles, the chief of which was love.

Even in the small amount of reasonably authentic teaching of Jesus that has survived, we have ample evidence to show why this most unusual person aroused antagonism—sufficient to bring about his death. The priests, the influential, and the highly respected people of his day were clearly very upset by his utterances. The religious authorities were incensed when he said of them, "Look out for the scholars who like to parade around in long robes and insist on being addressed properly in the marketplaces, and prefer important seats in the synagogues and the best couches at banquets."

Similarly, rich people were not all impressed when he said, "It's easier for a camel to squeeze through the eye of a needle than for a wealthy man to get into the kingdom of God!" Capitalists did not want to hear, "If you have money, don't lend it at interest. Rather give it to someone from whom you won't get it back." Indeed, even today wealthy Christians prefer to ignore these utterances.

Some of his teaching seemed to be so outrageous and ran so counter to everyday wisdom that a few people began to question his sanity. One tradition relates that his fellow townsmen thought he had gone mad, and tried to kill him. Further, the fact that Jesus frequently spoke about the coming of a new kind of kingdom was sufficient to put the Roman authorities on the alert and to see in him the danger of an insurrection that would threaten Roman rule. His teaching shows us why both Jewish and Roman authorities came to regard him as a public nuisance who had to be put out of the way. Had not John the Baptist, the original mentor of Jesus, already been beheaded for offending King Herod?

So, like Socrates who had been put to death for supposedly undermining public morality, Jesus was executed by one of the common methods of the day. Yet we lack sufficient documentation to know the exact reasons why the Romans executed Jesus. Weighty books are still being written to attempt to answer that question, for early Christian tradition soon tried to shift the blame from the Romans to the Jews. But whatever were the circumstances surrounding the crucifixion of Jesus, it helped to spark off the rise of Christianity and, within a short time, it caused the cross to become its most central symbol.

Still, the world of the following centuries would never have heard of the crucifixion of Jesus if it had not been for Paul. For that reason some claim, as we have already noted, that the latter was the actual founder of Christianity. Certainly he had by far the greatest influence on how it developed over the next twenty centuries. This means that a man who never met Jesus of Nazareth, nor even so much as heard him speak, in large measure shaped the Christian creeds.

JESUS AND CHRISTIAN ORTHODOXY

To what degree, then, does orthodox Christian doctrine truly reflect the teaching of the man long worshipped as the foundation of Christianity? In the Protestant Reformation of the sixteenth century the Reformers held the life and teaching of the church up to criticism in the light of what they found in the Bible. Five hundred years later, as a result of the revolution in biblical scholarship, we can now hold the Christian creeds up to criticism in the light of the original teaching of Jesus.

In the year 2000 the Westar Institute set out to explore the contours of a faith relevant to the global age we have entered in the third millennium. So its fall meeting was devoted to the theme of "The Once and Future Faith." To some extent this is what Bishop John Robinson was calling for in his book *A New Reformation?* written in 1966. And that was only three years after he had shocked the Christian world with his little book *Honest to God.* In his new book he raised the question of whether the church had become "an archaic and well-protected institution for the preservation of something that is irrelevant and incredible." He even suggested that the really significant movements of spiritual renewal were now taking place outside the church—and in spite of it.

The task of reforming Christian thought has proved very difficult because those who are committed to the defense of traditional Christianity have fiercely condemned the enterprise. Others, having concluded that Christian doctrine is so set in concrete that it cannot be reformed, have abandoned all affiliation with the Christian tradition. The once Christian world of the West is fast becoming polarized between these two extremes. However, the recovery of the voiceprints of the original Jesus has now opened up a middle way.

As soon as we reflect upon the original teachings of Jesus we find that the whole system of orthodox Christian doctrine that is now disintegrating is actually inconsistent with those teachings of

Jesus. Indeed, when examined in the light of the words of Jesus, it sometimes stands under moral condemnation,

The focal point of traditional Christian doctrine is Jesus Christ, the Son of God. He has been called the Savior not because of his teaching, but because of what he achieved by dying on the cross. His crucifixion was proclaimed as an event of cosmic proportions because it was interpreted as a divine sacrifice that brought forgiveness and salvation to sinful humankind. Christians proclaimed this message as the gospel—that is, the Good News—for in their view it saved sinners from eternal damnation and opened the door to eternal life in heaven.

The question of how Jesus' death on the cross achieved this goal gave rise to a variety of so-called theories of atonement. The earliest such theory interpreted the death of Jesus as the ransom paid by God to the Devil to rescue sinful humans from his clutches. A later theory avoided the reference to the Devil by interpreting the crucifixion in terms of moral bookkeeping. In this formulation Jesus acted on behalf of sinful humankind by repaying the debt we owed God for our sinful disobedience. This theory was later transformed into the theory of penal substitution, much beloved by evangelicals to this day. It states that since we all deserve to be punished for our sinful actions, and since God's sense of moral justice requires punishment to be suffered before he can forgive sins, then Jesus by his passion and crucifixion suffered that punishment on our behalf.

Today these theories of atonement have come under strong moral condemnation. Just as an ancient Israelite sage portrayed Job as the man who charged God with being immoral for allowing the innocent to suffer, so today our human ideals of justice and compassion are affronted by the idea that God should sacrifice his son. We are appalled at the very idea that any innocent person should be made to suffer for the wrongdoing of another. And the most serious condemnation of the various theories of atonement is found in the teaching of Jesus himself.

Take for example, the well-known parable of the prodigal son, which is certainly among the genuine sayings of Jesus. Preachers have often interpreted it as a kind of allegory of God's love for us his erring children. I remember pointing out to my fellow theological students more than sixty years ago that if this were such an allegory, it demonstrated that there was never any need for any atoning act by Jesus. It told how a father, though disappointed by his son's actions, was so overjoyed to see his erring son return that he welcomed him back immediately without any act of contrition.

Of course, the parable nowhere indicates it is intended as an allegory about God. It is about a human parent, and it provides strong approval for those mothers and fathers (of whom I have known several) who have continued to love their offspring to the end of their days in spite of being bitterly disappointed and even shamed by what their progeny have done. This is a parable about unconditional human love, love that does not demand to be repaid, love that continues to be shown even when no apology is forthcoming. If humans are capable of offering such unconditional love, how much more should a supposed heavenly Father display? This one parable of Jesus makes a mockery of the various theological attempts to see meaning in the death of Jesus by turning it into a salvation event of cosmic significance. It is not only the modern secular world that is causing the disintegration of orthodox Christian doctrine; the authentic words of Jesus themselves are doing so.

How is it then that the original teaching of Jesus became lost sight of and replaced by something else? And clearly the process was well under way in the first century. Perhaps someone who deplored this shift was the one who put into the mouth of Jesus, "Why do you call me 'Lord, Lord' and not do what I say?"

THE CHURCH IS NOT THE KINGDOM

A century ago one of the Catholic Modernists noted that "Jesus came proclaiming the coming of the kingdom of God, but what we got was the church!" Indeed, the chief topic in the teaching of Jesus—the kingdom of God—became so marginalized in Christian thought that the creeds make no mention of it at all. Instead, the creeds made the church an article of faith as expressed in the words of the creed, "I believe in one holy, catholic and apostolic church." As early as the end of the first century the author of Matthew's gospel was already putting into the mouth of Jesus words indicating that even during his ministry he intended to found a church: "On this rock (the faith of Peter) I will build my church."

We can now say with confidence that Jesus had no intention at all of founding a church—certainly not the kind of church that came to pass—any more than he claimed to be the Messiah or only Son of God. We have had some inkling of this for a century or more, but now that we have established a database of the words most likely to be the original utterances of Jesus, the gulf between what he said and what developed after his death has become even wider. We can reasonably surmise that Jesus would have been seriously shocked if he could have foreseen some of the things that would be said and done in his name.

What Jesus left behind him was not the church as it came to be, but a small community of his followers. Although similar communities spread, largely through the initial efforts of Paul, for the first three hundred years they did not even have their own buildings, but met in people's houses or in the catacombs when under persecution. Only after Constantine made it the state religion at the beginning of the fourth century did Christianity assume a more rigid institutional form and manifest itself to the world in the kind of public buildings we now call churches.

Then after the Fall of Rome in 410, the institution of the church began to take over some of the functions previously performed by the Roman State. That is how the church in the West gradually became such a powerful institution, one that could make even kings quake. The Pope took to himself one of the titles long borne by the Roman Emperor—Pontifex Maximus (the supreme bridge-builder). That is why we speak of the Pope's declarations to this day as "pontifical" statements.

Someone recently reminded me that in 1968 I wrote in *God in the New World*, "the church as we have known it in the past is destined to die and we must let it die. When Christianity takes to itself the forms and organization of the kingdoms of this world, it must expect those structures will suffer the same fate as those of man-made empires." Indeed, the power and authority wielded by the church through the centuries has been quite out of keeping with the teaching of Jesus. He said, "You know how those who rule over the Gentiles lord it over them and how the strong tyrannize the weak. It's not to be like that with you. Whoever wants to become great must be your servant. Whoever wants to be first must be your slave."

The institution of the church as a structure of power deserves to die, as it has been doing ever more rapidly in the last three hundred years. In spite of achieving many admirable things in its long life, the church developed a hierarchical and male-dominant character that is quite at variance with the teaching of Jesus. It is now losing its former authority by force of circumstances, instead of voluntarily surrendering that preeminence as it could have done if it had heeded the teaching of Jesus.

The institutional church will not disappear quickly even though it is seriously fragmented and growing weaker. Much less, however, will it disappear without a trace. The long-term influence and teaching of Jesus is already showing signs of outliving the church structures in which it has lived in the past. Just how that may be will be discussed in the next chapter, in which we shall explore the diverse futures of Christianity.

5

THE DIVERSE FUTURES
OF CHRISTIANITY

At the beginning of Chapter 2 I tried to show why Christianity is at a crossroads. I also suggested we should not think of Christianity as a set of unchangeable doctrines to be believed, but as a path of faith to be walked. The question of the future of Christianity then becomes "'Where will the Christian path of faith lead us from here?" But first we must observe that this is not the first crossroads reached in the Christian path of faith.

CHRISTIAN DIVERSITY, PAST AND PRESENT

We learn from the New Testament that the Christian path came to its first crossroad in the first century. Was the newly emerging Way to be confined within the parameters of Judaism or was it free to move into the Gentile world? Jesus' own brother James, along with most of the original disciples formed the community of Jerusalem Christians, and they opted for the Jewish Christian future. But these Jewish Christians were increasingly ostracized by Gentile Christians, and after about the fifth century they disappeared from view.

Thus the Christian path was directed by the Gentile Christians, yet not without dissension. A series of ecumenical councils only partially succeeded in providing clear and unifying boundaries to the Christian path of faith. In fact, they gave rise to three Christian paths, all of which exist to this day. After the Council of Chalcedon in 451, Christianity took a Nestorian path in Persia and China, a Coptic path in Egypt and Ethiopia, in addition to the Catholic or universal path in the rest of the then Christian world. The Christian West simply ignored the Copts and the Nestorians thereafter, and today most Christians in the West do not even know they exist. Christians went their three separate ways from that point because they could not agree on the Chalcedonian statement about the personhood of Jesus Christ, an abstruse formula that most Christians today do not even know, let alone understand.

Then came the Christian schism of 1054 when the Pope in Rome and the Patriarch of Constantinople excommunicated each other, partly over the issue of whether the Holy Spirit proceeds "from the Father and from the Son," or only from the Father. This division forced the main Christian path to divide into an Eastern Greek-based future and a Western Latin-based future.

A further parting of the ways occurred in Western Christianity in the sixteenth century, when the Protestant Reformation added several Protestant paths to the continuing Catholic path. It has taken four hundred years for Protestant and Catholic even to acknowledge one another as Christian. In the meantime the Catholic fear that Christianity would become even more divided once it forsook the unifying guardianship of the papacy has been amply justified. In the nineteenth century the choice of paths open to Protestant Christians multiplied further with the rise of the Plymouth Brethren, the Disciples of Christ, the Seventh Day Adventists, the Latter Day Saints, the Jehovah's Witnesses, Christian Scientists, and many others. This continued into the twentieth century with the Assemblies of God and many other Pentecostal movements.,

In the first half of the twentieth century the newly emerging ecumenical movement deplored the divisiveness manifested by Christians and tried to reverse the trend. Commendable though this was, it was doomed to failure, and with the gift of hindsight we can now see why. The reason is that every great religious tradition in its classical form manifests the tendency to diversify. The evolution of cultures conforms to the evolutionary tendency of all planetary life. Just as a genus divides into more and more species in the biological sphere, so a culture divides into more and more subcultures, some of which flourish while others die out.

Only when we begin to look at the history of religions and cultures as a whole does this become apparent. If we view any one tradition only from the inside (as we have normally done in Christianity) it appears to have an unchangeable essence—one that is to be preserved (or at times recovered) in its pristine purity. This is an illusion. Once we begin to understand religion in developmental or evolutionary terms, we see that there can be no one true and pure form of, say, Christianity, any more than there is one true form of mammal. Just as a family of species evolves out of the original biological genus, so out of primitive Christianity has evolved a family of different Christian species.

Also like biological species, cultures and religions come and go. As they do so, some elements often live on long afterwards in other traditions that they have influenced. We Christians still name the days of the week after the gods of Roman and Nordic religions long since dead. The word Easter preserves the name of the pagan goddess of spring. While only a tiny remnant of Zoroastrianism survived the spread of Islam in Iran, much more of it lives on in Judaism, Christianity and Islam, through its myth of the Last Judgment and other beliefs.

We need to be fully aware of the ever evolving and changing character of the human religious quest as we now turn to the future of the Judeo-Christian tradition as it enters the Second Axial Period. Not only is there already a great variety of Christian paths, but ever since Galileo these have felt threatened by the rise of the secular world. The once Christian West has become polarized. At one extreme is fundamentalism, moderating into various shades of traditional orthodoxy. At the other extreme is militant secularism, moderating into a post-Christian humanism. The term Christianity seems to refer to something much bigger and more alive than any of its particular forms, but for that very reason it is vague and difficult to define.

THE DIVERSE FUTURES OF CHRISTIANITY

If this Christianity is once again at the crossroads, its future is likely to be even more diverse than its past. What are these diverse futures?

First of all, the many and various Christian paths still being trodden will continue into the future, though some, like that of the Jewish Christians, will soon disappear. Although some Christians regard their own to be the only true Christian path, they are more inclined than in the past to acknowledge what they have in common. Catholicism, Eastern Orthodoxy, and the many forms of

Protestantism now show a surprising degree of sameness relative to the modern secular world. For example:

- They regard the Bible as divinely inspired and wholly reliable.
- They are suspicious of, and often reject, modern biblical scholarship.
- They believe God to be a personal being who responds to prayer.
- They worship Jesus Christ as the divine Son of God.
- They regard Christian orthodoxy as an unchangeable core of beliefs to which they must be faithful.

Thus traditional Christians judge the modern secular world to be a denial of the true faith and an enemy to be held at bay and eventually defeated. This has become the Achilles heel of Christian orthodoxy. As King Canute is said to have commanded the waves to retreat, Christian orthodoxy expects the secular world to conform to its pattern of truth. Its claim to possess the ultimate truth shows that it has now become blind to much if not all new truth. This means that in the post-Copernican, post-Darwinian secular world that we have now entered, the only future for Christian orthodoxy is as a museum piece. This is because Christian orthodoxy has seriously misunderstood the origin and nature of the secular world.

Although the secular world may legitimately be judged post-Christian, it is not anti-Christian. After all, it emerged out of the Christian West, is a product of the Christian West, and is motivated by the values, aspirations and visions of its matrix. The modern secular world is all part of a continually evolving cultural process. Just as the original Christians claimed the Christian Way or path of faith was the legitimate continuation and fulfillment of the Jewish path, so it may be claimed that the modern, secular, and humanistic world is the legitimate continuation of the Judeo-Christian path of faith.

It is salutary to remember what occurred while the newly emerging Christianity, then still in a fluid state, was taking shape within Hellenistic culture. The second-century Christian thinkers known as the Apologists claimed that everything that was true in Greek culture was also part and parcel of Christianity. They even claimed

Plato as a Christian. Similarly, we should be saying that everything we find to be true in the modern world as a result of the knowledge explosion is part and parcel of developing Christianity. In order to specify the chief phases through which it has passed, we should perhaps refer to Christianity as the Judeo-Christian-secular path of faith.

But though Christian orthodoxy would lead us down a blind road that has no exit, we can still learn a valuable lesson from it. If we are going to find a satisfactory path of faith that will lead into the global future, we need to study our cultural past to understand who we are, how we got to where we are, and how we came to discern the supreme human values that still lay a claim on us. Those who turn their backs entirely on Christianity in all its forms and refuse to acknowledge our common indebtedness to the cultural matrix out of which the modern world has emerged are cutting themselves off from their cultural and spiritual roots. As plants without roots wither and die, so do cultures that forget their past. The study of the past illuminates the present but it does not dictate the future. That is why the Bible remains an invaluable set of documents. We learn much from it, but it is not a straitjacket we are bound by.

THE SECULAR WORLD AND THE CHRISTIAN FUTURE

Having acknowledged the necessity for Christianity to remember its biblical past, we must now turn to the secular world in which Christianity finds its real future. To appreciate this we have only to look at some of the values highly prized in the modern secular world. One of them is personal freedom. The pursuit of human freedom has been a central motif in the Judeo-Christian tradition since Moses led the Israelites out of slavery. It went a stage further when Jesus opened the door to another kind of freedom: freedom from the cultural and religious compulsions from the past. Even Paul gloried in this, exclaiming to his Galatian converts, "You were called to freedom," and the Fourth Gospel put into the mouth of Jesus, "You shall know the truth and the truth will make you free."

With the coming of the modern world, however, the pursuit of freedom has flourished as never before, starting with the freedom to think for oneself and to pursue the truth. These were quickly followed by the freedom to speak and to publish. The result was a whole series of emancipations: the democratic emancipation from absolute monarchy, the emancipation of slaves, the emancipation of women from male domination, the emancipation of the humankind from racist prejudice, and currently the emancipation of homosexuals from homophobia. Sadly, the churches have often been initially opposed to these emancipations; no longer on the side of freedom, they committed themselves to the dogmas of the past.

Values such as freedom, love, justice, and the pursuit of peace were once dominant in the Judeo-Christian tradition. They now continue in the secular world but no longer need the support of divine authority. Their own inherent power to convince us of their worth has replaced the sanctions of the now departing deity. Indeed, those people who love their fellows because they are convinced of the value of love show greater moral maturity than those who love only because they are commanded by a higher authority.

That is why this new cultural age has been called "humankind's coming of age." Just as attaining adulthood means that one must leave behind the security of parental control and take responsibility for his or her own actions, so the human race must now learn how to practice love, justice, and peaceful co-existence because it recognizes their inherent value, and not out of fear of Hell or the reward of Heaven.

But "humankind's coming of age" also means that individuals are freer to choose their way of life or path of faith. This is why we have come to value diversity more than conformity. The conformity of belief and practice so dominant in the past made heresy the most heinous of sins. "Heresy," derived from a Greek word that means "choice," is used in the New Testament to refer to a belief system of those who have the audacity to choose their own way of life rather than follow that of the majority. As Peter Berger pointed out in his book *The Heretical Imperative*, modernity has brought to human life an extraordinary expansion in available choices. This is true not only in the supermarket, but much more important in the area of religious belief and practice. We are now free to choose our personal way of life; we do so from a veritable smorgasbord of options. In today's free and open society the exercise of personal choice is not merely permitted but has become a necessity. We are all forced to be choosers—that is, heretics! Even fundamentalists today are choosers (or heretics) in that they choose to believe that the Bible is literally the Word of God.

Of course the new freedom to choose our way of life brings no guarantee that we shall make wise choices. Just as many an adolescent goes off the rails on reaching adulthood, the danger becomes greatly magnified when the whole human species comes of age and becomes free from the cultural restraints of the past. Now that the moral life has become personalized as never before and we are challenged to make new moral decisions and work out our own solutions to the problems of life, many of us fall by the wayside. Too often people selfishly engage in anti-social behavior. Too often people abandon one form of superstition only to adopt another. While this is all too true, we must not allow it to blind us to the many aspects of social life in the secular world that display a much more mature morality than that found in the Christendom of the past.

THE CONTINUITY OF CHRISTIANITY IN THE SECULAR WORLD

Can the secular world really be the offspring of the Christian West if it so clearly abandons the figure of Christ as the divine Son of God? Other than in the values just mentioned, can we discover any continuity between the Christian past and the secular present?

First, we need to acknowledge that the pioneers of the modern secular world were all thinkers deeply immersed in the Christian tradition. The first sign of the Second Axial Age is to be found in the love of the natural world shown by St. Francis. Then we may point to the teaching of the Franciscan philosopher, William of Ockham (1300–1349), an intellectual system labeled the "Via Moderna"— the Modern Way. It flourished among the Renaissance humanists, the Protestant Reformers, and the thinkers of the Enlightenment.

No one of the pioneering creators of the modern world—including such figures as Erasmus, Luther, and John Locke—ever thought of himself as departing from the Christian tradition.

Second, we need to understand the radical nature of the central Christian doctrine of the incarnation. This proclaims that the divine reality has been enfleshed within the human condition. This was an extraordinary assertion when first made; it early on offended Jews and Muslims, and still does. They defend pure monotheism , which asserts an unbridgeable gulf between deity and humanity.

Of course Christian orthodoxy eventually confined the assertion of the incarnation to a single instance: the man Jesus who came to be viewed as the Christ. But in its earliest years Christian thought was much more fluid than that. Paul spoke of Christ as the New Adam. He meant that Christ was to embody the whole human race just as the first Adam embodied the whole human race. That is why Paul spoke of all Christians as being "in Christ." In his view Christians are new creatures—new beings—for they participate in the incarnation of the divine. Unfortunately, as traditional Christian teaching increasingly emphasized the divinity of Jesus to the virtual exclusion of his humanity, Christians lost sight of the wider implications of the assertion of incarnation.

It was not until biblical scholars like David Strauss set in motion the deconstruction of the Christ figure and the recovery of the true humanity of Jesus that it became possible for people like Ludwig Feuerbach to expound what he took to be the "True Meaning of the Incarnation." It meant that all the qualities previously associated with the divine being were henceforth to become enfleshed within humanity.

Similarly, the Anglican theologian J. R. Illingworth as long ago as 1891 was warning Christians not to regard secular thought as the enemy of Christianity. In an essay on the incarnation he said, "Secular civilization has co-operated with Christianity to produce the modern world. It is nothing less than the providential correlative and counterpart of the incarnation." This central doctrine of Christian faith has thus played a role in promoting the emergence of the modern secular world out of the Christian past. In today's terminology the incarnation may be described as the humanization of God, the secularization of the divine, and the earthing of heaven.

Furthermore, a new kind of god-talk is taking the place of the old, and herein also lies continuity. Just as the Jews retained their word for god but gave it a new meaning, so in this Second Axial Period, god-talk is playing a new role. This phenomenon has its roots in the biblical tradition itself—its reference to "the god of Israel," "the god of Abraham," "my god," and "your god." Of course "the god of Abraham" was invisible, so if one were to ask, "How can I learn about the god of Abraham?" the appropriate answer would be, "See how Abraham lived his life. Try to understand what motivated him at the deepest level. That is all you will ever know of the god of Abraham." Similarly, god-talk in the secular world means referring to the values we live by and the goals we aspire to.

In the modern secular world the supernatural/natural dichotomy has been swallowed up and eliminated. The almost infinite physical universe is itself awe-inspiring and full of mystery. The supernatural force once conceived as the objective personal God has disappeared from reality. What has survived from traditional god-talk are the values that were the attributes of God such as love, compassion, and justice. Even the New Testament says "God is love," and Jesus himself exhorted us to enflesh the divine values when he said, "You must be as completely good as is your Father in heaven." The fact that we may now refer to those values as human values and find some of them highly honored in other cultural traditions does not make them any less valid or important.

To illustrate the continuing relationship between the secular world and its Christian past, I shall sketch the outlines of the path of faith into the secular global future. To do so I take three themes that are basic to the Judeo-Christian tradition.

FAITH

The first theme is faith. Every cultural tradition is a path of faith. The Bible itself emphasizes this when it starts with the figure of Abraham. In these days of increasing contact between the Christian and Islamic worlds it is salutary to remember that the figure of

Abraham is equally important to the faith traditions of Judaism, Christianity, and Islam. Jews honor Abraham as the father of their nation. Christians honor Abraham as a model of faith. Muslims honor Abraham as the first Muslim.

But what made Abraham a model man of faith? It was the fact that he showed trust when he heeded the voice he heard and (as the New Testament says) went out not knowing where he was to go. He had no map. He had no Torah, no Bible, and no Qur'an to guide him. The midrashic Jewish legends tell that Abraham even smashed his father's idols before setting on his journey. Faith requires us to surrender attachment to all tangibles. For the journey of faith we must be free of all excess baggage.

The Judeo-Christian tradition has on many occasions found itself so weighed down by its accumulating lore and mythology that it has had to jettison its excess baggage. The Protestant Reformers abandoned a great deal of what had accumulated in medieval Christianity, including the belief in Purgatory. The Second Axial Period requires us to jettison a great deal more than the Protestant Reformers did—including a post-mortem heaven and hell, a divine savior, an objective personal deity, the doctrine of the atonement, and the whole system of dogma that envelops them. These doctrines were once important as the expression of faith in a worldview where they were appropriate. That worldview has now become obsolete, and in the modern world these doctrines have become a hindrance to faith.

Faith is not dependent on belief in a personal God or in any particular object. In common human experience faith is multi-faceted and operates at a variety of levels. That is why in various secular contexts we may be exhorted to put faith in ourselves, in our ideas, in other people, in the natural world. It is up to us to clarify for ourselves just what we most deeply revere and to recognize with Martin Luther that whatever we put our trust in becomes our God. We have to learn throughout life to distinguish between idols and the God we can truly trust. In the context of the modern worldview, the theistic God has become a superstitious and idolatrous object.

Today we are becoming acutely aware of our dependence on the earth. That remarkable Christian visionary and scientist, Teilhard de Chardin, was so awestruck by what he had learned of the self-evolving universe that he once said:

> If, as the result of some interior revolution, I were to lose in succession my faith in Christ, my faith in a personal God, and my faith in spirit, I feel that I should continue to believe invincibly in the world. The world . . . is the first, the last and the only thing in which I believe. It is by this faith that I live.

In this ecologically sensitive age, that is a good place to begin. The evolution of life on this planet is an awe-inspiring mystery, and it was what Teilhard had come to understand as God. As we have seen, Jesus the sage drew attention to the marvels of nature to encourage people to walk the path of faith. The capacity of nature to create new forms and to renew life is more breathtaking than any of the unusual events commonly called miracles. Faith is a matter of being open to the marvels of the natural world and of saying "Yes!" to life and all that it offers.

HOPE

The second theme is hope. This is as basic to the human condition as is faith. "Hope springs eternal in the human breast," said Alexander Pope. Where hope dies, faith grows weak, for the two are closely allied.

The experience of hope has played a dominant role in the long history of the Judeo-Christian tradition. Abraham looked forward to a city with foundations. Moses looked for a land flowing with milk and honey. The Babylonian exiles hoped for the restoration of the Kingdom of David. Christians looked for the coming of the Kingdom of God, those very words becoming permanently captured in the Lord's Prayer: "Thy Kingdom come." In the course of time, however, this hope became transformed into a post-mortem personal destiny in heaven, which even became known theologically as the Christian Hope.

The coming of the secular world has brought us back to earth again, so that something like the original intention of "the Kingdom of God" becomes relevant once more. Our chief hopes for the future are much more this-worldly than were those of our forbears. Individually, of course, we hope for a long and healthy life. Collectively, we hope for social harmony, for economic prosperity, and for international peace. More recently our hope has incorporated the conservation of the earth's ecology.

Hope must not be confused with blind optimism. As I have tried to show in my book *The World to Come*, the century we have just entered is presenting us with so many frightening challenges that it is becoming quite difficult to hold out hope for a better world. Yet, as theologian Jürgen Moltmann has said, "It is just because we cannot know whether humanity is going to survive or not, we have to act today as if the future of the whole of humanity depended on us."

LOVE

My third theme from the Bible is love. There has always been general agreement that love is central to the Judeo-Christian tradition. Jesus named as the two primary commandments injunctions selected from the Jewish Scriptures: "You shall love the Lord your God with all your heart and mind and strength," and "You shall love your neighbor as yourself."

But Jesus went further than anything in the Jewish tradition. He said, "Love your enemies." It is sadly ironic that throughout Christian history the most original dictum in the whole teaching of Jesus is just what Christians have found most difficult to carry out. Not only have professing Christians been little better than anybody else in loving their enemies, but even the centrality of love itself became repositioned. Christian orthodoxy constructed a divine savior so that we sinners would become the object of his love. The original message of love, which exhorted us to save others, became distorted into one of exploiting it to secure our own salvation.

The secular world has no problem with acknowledging the importance of loving one's fellow humans. It sometimes even criticizes the church for lack of love shown towards those who do not agree with it. The secular world acknowledges that love should not only cross ethnic and religious boundaries but should extend to all planetary forms of life. The secular world can readily affirm the slogan "Love conquers all" and, if it uses god-language at all, could say "God is love." The secular world can even agree with Paul, the first Christian theologian, who wrote, "Three things have lasting value—faith, hope, and love; and the greatest of them all is love."

Is Christianity going anywhere? The short answer is that Orthodox Christianity will undoubtedly survive for quite some time in many of its traditional forms. Some will rejoice in finding spiritual fulfillment in one or more of them. Nevertheless, Christian orthodoxy is not going anywhere; at best it is simply standing still. To people living in the secular world, Christian orthodoxy has lost credibility. Those who insist on expounding it as the answer to the world's problems have become blind guides; and as Jesus said, "If a blind person guides a blind person, they will both fall into the ditch."

The real future of the Judeo-Christian path of faith is a secular one. Far from being the enemy of Christianity, the truly secular life is the legitimate continuation of the Judeo-Christian tradition. The traditional worship of God has widened into the celebration of life. Faith is a matter of saying "Yes!" to life in all of its planetary complexity. Even while shedding many of Christianity's past symbols and creedal formulations, the secular path still honors the abiding values it has learned from its Christian origins. Concerned as it is with the pursuit of truth, the practice of justice, and the nurture of compassion, freedom, and peace, the secular world is learning to live by faith, hope, and love. Faith requires us to be free of all excess baggage. Hope requires us to be open to an ever-evolving future. Love requires us to be inclusive of all people and all cultural traditions.

THE GREENING OF CHRISTIANITY

6

THE GLOBAL CRISIS

During the twentieth century three words all linked to the same Greek root began to capture our attention. The Greek word was *oikos*, meaning "household," "dwelling," "home." The rise to prominence of these three words reflects how we humans are becoming increasingly conscious of the global home we share.

- **Ecumenical** came from *oikos* by way of the Greek word *oikumene*, which means "the whole world that humankind inhabits as its home."
- **Economic** came from *oikos* by way of the Greek word *oikonomia*, which means "the law of the household" or "household management."
- **Ecological** also came from *oikos*, but more indirectly.

The word ecology was coined by a German zoologist, Ernst Haeckel, who used the term *oekologie* to mean the relation of an animal to both its organic and inorganic environment. Thus ecology deals with organisms and their home environments, and has been defined variously as "the study of the interrelationships of organisms with their environment and each other" and as "the biology of ecosystems."

In the course of the twentieth century we became increasingly familiar with these three words. In the first half of the century the word "ecumenical" became widely used to describe the attempt by many Christians to re-establish the essential unity of the worldwide Christian church after it had been increasingly fragmented following the Protestant Reformation.

Then, as the cultural phenomenon of globalization began to gather force after World War II, economics grew in importance as the study of understanding and managing material affairs, first those of our national household and, more recently, in what is called macro-economics, those of our global household.

In the last third of the twentieth century our growing awareness of the ecological character of all life on earth awakened us to impending planetary crises, disruptions for which we humans, whether out of ignorance or willful self-centeredness, are largely responsible.

Since St. Andrew's Trust was established to study the interaction between religion and society, this series of lectures has been planned to explore what impact our new understanding of ecology will have on the Judeo-Christian tradition. To what extent, if any, does it require Christian thought and practice to undergo change? As we shall find, that impact is so far-reaching that these lectures could well have been titled "The Transition from Theo-logy to Eco-logy." We start now with "The Global Crisis."

A GATHERING STORM

Today scientists, historians, and other commentators warn us of a global ecological crisis. This has the potential to be even more devastating and long-lasting than a thermonuclear war, for it could mean the end of all life as we know it. The crisis they point to has been growing for some time; at first it was quite unobtrusive, but recently its accelerating effects have become alarming.

The first hint of it that I recall came when I was a rural parish minister in North Otago in the early 1940's. Farmers were being warned that improper use of their land was causing soil erosion of such serious degree that it could lead to disastrous results. I remember how some farmers took strong objection to being told what they could or could not do with their own land. That was an early indication of how many people react today, as more and more information comes to light about the irreversible damage that we humans are inflicting on the very earth we depend upon for life.

A FIRST CLEAR CRY — AND
RECENT ECHOES . . .

1962 saw the publication of a prophetic book. Its author, Rachel Carson, was an aquatic biologist who had already established a worldwide reputation for her books on the sea, but today she is chiefly remembered for *Silent Spring*. Although it became a best seller and is credited with creating a worldwide awareness of the dangers of environmental pollution, her suggestion that synthetic pesticides were doing more harm than good caused many to dismiss her book as "so much hogwash." Her death in 1964 prevented her from seeing her allegations confirmed, the banning of many pesticides, and the rapid spread of organic farming.

The last three decades have seen an ever-increasing number of books warning that a frightening nemesis is now appearing on the horizon as a result of our changing relationship with the earth. Their titles commonly proclaim the gravity of the problem: *The Fate of the Earth* (Jonathan Schell, 1982); *The Dream of the Earth* (Thomas Berry, 1988); *The Crisis of Life on Earth* (Tim Radford, 1990); *Earth in the Balance* (Al Gore, 1993); *The Sacred Balance* (David Suzuki, 1997); and *Five Holocausts* (Derek Wilson, 2001).

These modern secular prophets are alerting us to the early warning signals coming from a planet now feeling dire pressure from the activities of the human species. What may be called the humanization of the earth is leading to an imminent global crisis. Our species is now in the process of destroying in a few decades a life-support system that took millions of years to evolve. Some of these prophets are so pessimistic that they question whether it is possible for some six to eight billion people to change the direction of our global life sufficiently in the relatively short time left in which to do it.

Others are more hopeful and see no reason why, with human ingenuity and the latest technology, we should not be able to reverse the dangerous trends we have already set in motion. Jonathan Schell ends *The Fate of the Earth* by pointing out that humankind must make a choice between the path that leads to death and the path that leads to life. His words are reminiscent of the ancient challenge of Moses: "I have set before you this day life and good, death and evil . . . therefore choose life."

. . . FALLING ON DEAF EARS

But how many today understand that we face a choice between life and death on a global scale? The large masses of the earth's population are almost completely ignorant of the larger picture. They are so caught up with what goes on in their own little worlds that they are as yet unaware of what the prophets are saying, let alone able or concerned to judge or act upon their prophecies. A significant proportion of these inhabit the third-world countries of Africa, India, and South America, and can be excused for their ignorance on the grounds that all of their energy and thinking is taken up with the need to scratch out a living.

Much more serious is the ignorance or apathy to be found among those in the first and second worlds whose affluent life styles are chiefly responsible for the crisis. There too, most people are so taken up with personal and local affairs of the moment that they either remain largely unaware of the crisis or feel helpless to make any difference. It is there also that we find the vigorous critics who dismiss the prophetic voices as "doom merchants," purveyors of unrest who grossly exaggerate the warning signs and ignore the capacity of human ingenuity to respond positively to them. These critics are people whose wealth, business interests, and economic policies are dependent upon the very technology currently doing the damage. Largely driven by acquisitiveness, they appear to have shut their eyes to the consequences of their own self-interest.

A MUFFLED DETONATION . . .

What is it we should all be more aware of? First and perhaps foremost is the population explosion. It has been estimated that at the beginning of the Christian era the human population of the earth was some 300 million. Population growth remained relatively slow, so that by 1750 it had reached only about 800 million. Disease, epidemics, famine, and high mortality among children always took their toll. But that has now been drastically changed by such otherwise beneficial developments as medical science, education in personal hygiene, better sanitation, and improved economic conditions.

Population growth has steadily accelerated since 1750. By 1800 the world population had reached one billion, and it had taken some two million years to do so. But by 1930 it had doubled to two billion. A third billion was added by 1960, a fourth by 1974, the fifth before 1990, and the sixth by 1998. During the twentieth century the human population of the earth quadrupled, and this in spite of the tens of millions who died from world wars or epidemics.

. . . BECOMES A SUPER-BOMB

Present projections estimate that the global population will have reached eight billion people by 2025. We currently add the equivalent of another London every month and another China every fifteen years. We see this expansion only from the human point of view, but relative to all the other animals, the human species has suddenly expanded like a plague of locusts, and is eating them out of house and home.

Since the size of the planet remains the same, the increase in human population forces people to live more closely together. In 1800 only 3 per cent of the world's population lived in urban areas. By 1900 it had grown to 13 per cent and this had reached 50 per cent by 2000. This trend not only produces slums, but means that many fewer people have first-hand experience of the earth and the way it produces our food. This fact, coupled with the rapid process of modern globalization, means that humans are becoming increasingly dependent upon one another for their well-being and basic sustenance, so that any upset has increasingly disastrous ramifications.

Until the 1950's the debate about human numbers remained largely academic. When artificial forms of contraception were coming into common use in the first half of the twentieth century, some people vigorously opposed them on religious grounds, regarding their use as purely a matter of personal morality. Now that the global population is reaching the limits of sustainability on the earth, contraception has become a social concern as well as a personal one. The Roman Catholic rejection of all artificial forms of contraception and the still widespread moral condemnation of clinical abortion show that traditional morality is sadly out of touch with today's moral problems.

COLLATERAL DAMAGE

The population explosion is also drastically altering the racial composition of the world's population. For example, in 1950 the population of Africa was only half that of Europe, but by 2025 it could well be three times that of Europe. By the year 2025 Nigeria's population could jump from 113 to 301 million, Kenya's from 25 to 77 million, Tanzania's from 27 to 84 million, and Zaire's from 36 to 99 million. This means that nations already economically depressed, and in many cases saddled with massive international debt, will bear the burden of feeding between two and three times as many more mouths than they do at present. This predicament is setting the scene for a pandemic of unthinkable proportions.

A massive rise in population means a gigantic increase in the demands being made on the earth to provide the necessities of life—water, food, clothing, housing. Modern agricultural science and new technologies have made possible a great increase in food production. That is the positive side. Indeed the affluent countries have never been so well fed. But the radical imbalance in global wealth has meant increasing hunger in third world countries, most of them the very countries where the population is expanding fastest. Perhaps with more willingness to share the fruits of the earth and more efficient means of distributing food we could feed the global population adequately. But while this sanguine hope is continually promoted, it shows no signs of fulfillment. And even this argument will soon become invalid if we do not find a means of stabilizing the population of the globe.

THE BEST-LAID PLANS . . .

But increasing food production to meet the needs of an expanding population has had some dangerous ancillary effects that may cumulatively spell disaster on the grand scale. To make the point quickly, I shall present the chain of cause and effect in a somewhat simplistic manner.

- To meet the basic needs of an expanding population we must increase the food supply.

- To achieve this, agricultural science has come to depend on artificial fertilizers and pesticides, some of which have negative side effects.
- To house more people we must build more cities.
- To build more cities we must gobble up valuable agricultural land.
- To replace the land thus lost, as well as breaking in even more agricultural land to meet the increased food requirements, we destroy the forests. (The earth's forests are shrinking by 42 million acres per year, the rain forest of the Amazon valley being the prime example.)
- By destroying the rainforests and other surface vegetation we are losing productive land by washing vast amounts of topsoil into the sea. The United States alone is reported to be losing four to six billion tons annually.
- But the rainforests, by absorbing carbon dioxide and releasing oxygen, have been instrumental in keeping in balance the atmospheric gases necessary for life.
- The increased level of carbon dioxide in the atmosphere as a result of the greatly increased burning of fossil fuels is now causing the phenomenon of global warming.
- Global warming is changing our weather patterns, bringing extremes of both storms and droughts, and thus seriously reducing food production.
- Global warming will soon cause the icecaps to melt and the sea levels to rise, endangering the homes of hundreds of millions who live close to sea level.
- A number of our inventions and activities have had the effect of depleting the ozone layer, which protects us from the harmful effects of the sun's radiation. This not only increases the incidence of malignant cancers but can also bring about unforeseen genetic changes.

. . . CAN GO ASTRAY

It was not until the twentieth century that the effects of such human factors as the population expansion and human technology began to rival natural forces. Together they are now sufficient to compromise the natural conditions of the surface of the planet. We are not only causing the extinction of many other species by destroying their natural habitats; we are endangering our own habitat by polluting air and water, the two most basic elements on which our existence depends.

The chain of causes linking these unfortunate phenomena is an example of the interconnectedness of all life on this planet. It vividly illustrates the reason why we had to create the new term "ecology." We are coming to have such a radically new understanding of all life on this planet that the term "biosphere," coined less than a century ago, is now being replaced by "ecosphere."

Just as we have come to understand each organism internally as a complex living system, so also each species of organism constitutes with its natural environment a larger living system, which could be called a "life field." Thus all forms of planetary life are both involved in and dependent on systems. The ecosphere is a complex system of systems within systems, and is itself dependent on the energy of the sun.

WANTED: EQUILIBRIUM

The continuing life of each species depends upon the preservation of the delicate balance that has evolved between the organism and the environment that supports it. Each organism contains self-regulating mechanisms that help to preserve that balance. We can understand this better by thinking of the organism we know best—the human being. We have long been accustomed to think of ourselves as wholes, rather than as aggregations of parts. Indeed, it is only modern physiology that has fully identified the various organs, glands, and immune systems that exist within the human body and promote its well-being. When one or more of those systems has its balance disturbed and can no longer function (as, say, in diabetes) our health (literally, our "wholeness") suffers. We become ill and, if the balance cannot be restored, we die.

The earth both provides certain basic necessities and imposes certain requirements for the survival of all its creatures. Humans have evolved within those parameters. Our respiratory system is suited to both the nature and the proportions of the gases found in the atmosphere. Our bodies, which are 80 per cent water, reflect the earth's abundant supply of that vital liquid. The ozone layer protects us from the sun's harmful radioactivity. Our muscles and bone structure have evolved to meet the conditions of the earth's gravitational pull. For humans to be healthy they must be able to breathe fresh air, drink clean water, eat adequate food, and live in an environment not too different from that in which they became human. They must even keep to a diet not too different from that of their ancestors going back tens of thousands of years. The more the environment changes from that in which a species has evolved, the more the health and behavior of that species will show maladjustment. If the change is great enough, the health of the species will deteriorate to the point of extinction. We humans will always be earthlings, and like all other earthly creatures our existence depends upon our mother earth.

The fast-increasing human population has not only put added strain on the natural resources of the earth; more seriously, it has upset the ecological balance between various species and their sources of sustenance. By our sudden expansion in numbers, we humans are interfering with the food chains that have evolved over time; this means that we are depriving many other creatures of sustenance to the point where their extinction will signal the possibility of a similar fate for us. All food for human consumption, as well as that for many other species, comes either directly or indirectly from four ecological systems: croplands, grasslands, forests, and fisheries. And each of these is being seriously depleted by a rapidly growing human population.

More than a dozen years ago 1575 distinguished scientists, including more than half of all living Nobel Laureates, signed a document that warned of the dire threat to western civilization in the foreseeable future and appealed for help from industries, businesses, and religious organizations. During the last four years 1300 scientists from 95 countries have produced a report

entitled *Millennium Ecosystems Assessment*, which concludes that
the human race has so ruinously squandered the earth's natural
resources during the last fifty years that the planet has been over-
drawn, thereby saddling our descendants with an environmental
debt of staggering proportions.

CHRISTIANITY AND CRISIS

How shall Christianity—which has always claimed to be concerned
with the salvation of humankind—respond to this global ecological
crisis? This is a question we must now explore.

In the light of what was said earlier, it may seem odd that
the idea of an imminent global catastrophe is not at all new for
Christianity. On the contrary, such an expectation permeates the
New Testament. In his earliest letters Paul referred to the imminent
coming of wide and sudden destruction that would arrive without
warning like a thief in the night. Early Christians believed the end
of the world would come in their own lifetime—they referred to
it as the *eschaton*, or end-time—and preached the Gospel as the
answer to that dire threat. Paul and others declared that when
in the last days the global catastrophe struck, Jesus Christ would
return in glory and establish his everlasting kingdom. Only those
who responded to the Gospel would be saved.

Many current New Testament scholars have cast doubt on
whether this concern with the end-time was a part of the original
teaching of Jesus; but in any case it certainly played a prominent
role in Christianity from the time of Paul onwards. It may well
have been one of the factors contributing to the rapid spread of
Christianity in the latter half of the first century. It is noteworthy
that the first three Gospels, written some twenty to fifty years
after Paul, placed conspicuous and vivid warnings of the coming
eschaton in the mouth of Jesus. In Mark we find him warning of
tribulation shortly to come on a scale unknown since the beginning
of time: the sun would be darkened, the moon would lose its light,
the stars would fall from the sky, and heaven and earth would pass
away. In Luke, Jesus is said to have likened the imminent crisis to

the Great Flood that reportedly wiped out nearly all of planetary life in the time of Noah.

Once this expectation of a world crisis became incorporated into Gospels that were later raised to the status of Holy Writ, it gained a permanent role in the Christian tradition. Of course Christian interest in it has waxed and waned through the centuries. A striking example is the fact that St. John's Gospel, written at the end of the first century, seems to have ignored it. Indeed, some scholarly interpreters have regarded this last Gospel as a fresh interpretation of the Christian message, one especially written for the time after the first wave of expectation had passed. One such scholar described its central theme as "realized eschatology, " a term by which he indicated the Gospel's assumption that the *eschaton* had already come—that Jesus had already returned, but not in the way originally expected; rather he was now present spiritually in the life of the church.

But even if that were the Fourth Gospel's intention, it could hardly erase the early convictions about an imminent end-time and the hope for the return of Jesus Christ, since these remained in the earlier Gospels and were subsequently spelled out in the Creeds. This fact in itself was enough to ensure that from time to time throughout Christian history resurgences of this eschatological expectation have occurred. In the nineteenth century, nearly all the many Protestant sects that arose on the basis of biblical literalism focused on the imminent end of the world and the return of Jesus. Jehovah's Witnesses still make much of it, and Seventh Day Adventists even included this hope of the Second Coming in their name.

Curiously enough, when modern methods of studying the Bible began to emerge a little over 200 years ago, scholars at first took little notice of this element in the New Testament. It was not until just over a century ago that Johannes Weiss and Albert Schweitzer alerted biblical scholars to what then became known as the eschatological strand in the New Testament. Awareness of it came as a severe jolt to the liberal theologians of the day, for they found it difficult to reconcile these end-time expectations with much traditional theology, to say nothing of modern religious thought. The branch of academic theology known as "eschatology" had long focused its attention on the eternal destiny of the individual rather than on the destiny of the earth; so since the beginning of the twentieth century the liberal theologians have generally concluded that the eschatological expectations embedded in the New Testament were simply part of the mythical thinking of the ancient world, ideas that had now become outmoded.

THE RISE OF A DANGEROUS COUNTER-CURRENT

But such an interpretation does not satisfy those who read the Bible literally. They take the New Testament references to the "last days" very seriously. This is why, as fundamentalism has spread during the twentieth century, and is even moving into some mainline churches, we encounter the most widespread manifestation of end-of-the-world thinking to be found among Christians since the religion's earliest days. According to a Time-CNN poll taken in 2002, 59 percent of Americans believe that the prophecies found in the book of Revelation are about to come true—and nearly one-quarter to think the Bible actually predicted the 9/11 attacks. This explains why the best-selling books in America today are the twelve volumes of the "Left Behind" series written by the Christian fundamentalist Timothy LaHaye. By relating the words of the Bible to current events in the Middle East, he has prophesied a scenario of the future that has captivated the imagination of millions of Americans.

Here is a sketch. Israel will shortly occupy the rest of the lands long ago given to it by God. It will then be attacked by the legions of the antichrist—presumably the Arab nations and Russia. This will lead to the final showdown, biblically known as the battle of Armageddon. The messiah will return for the "rapture," the process by which true believers will be lifted up from the earth and transported to Heaven. From their grandstand seat they will watch the fate of those "left behind." These latter will suffer years of tribulation, after which the righteous will enter Heaven with the Son of God, while sinners will be condemned to eternal hellfire.

To all reasonably thoughtful people living in the modern world this whole scenario is so preposterous as to be quite laughable. We *could* afford to ignore it were not the people buying these books the very ones who put George Bush back into the White House. They also lend strong moral support to Israel and the Jewish settlements in the West Bank and back it up with money. Far from fearing war with Islam, they welcome any future Christian-Islamic conflict as a necessary step on the road that will bring them final redemption. They see the invasions of Iraq and Afghanistan as warm-up acts. Iran may be next. This is a message that over 1600 Christian radio stations and 250 Christian TV stations in the United States broadcast continually.

AN OMINOUS CONCURRENCE

The two very different apocalyptic pictures I have outlined—the ecological and the biblical—constitute a tragic irony. At the very time when the Christian community is being challenged to direct its energies to the real ecological crisis now looming, its fundamentalist wing is giving its attention to a mythical global crisis expected two thousand years ago. It is worrisome enough that fundamentalist Christians in the world's most powerful nation have become such a significant force that they can endanger international peace; it is truly alarming that their vision of a coming Armageddon is blinding them and others to the real problem we face—the ecological crisis.

It is their misuse of the Bible that has led fundamentalists astray. Certainly the Bible records numerous warnings issued by the ancient prophets; but they were speaking not to us, but to the people of their own times. It is salutary to recall that Jesus rebuked the religious people of his day for failing "to interpret the signs of the times." It has been left largely to prophets outside of the churches to read the signs of the times in our day. Many Christian fundamentalists not only reject and even despise today's secular prophets, but show no interest at all in the many environmental initiatives now being launched in an attempt to respond positively to the ecological crisis. Since the great majority of Christian fundamentalists live in the United States, it is no accident that this most powerful nation not only rejects such international protocols as the Kyoto agreements, but undertakes actions that directly endanger world peace.

Perhaps the most striking example of the fundamentalist mindset is James Gaius Watt, who as Secretary of the Interior in the Reagan administration advocated giving developers access to national parks and natural resources. His argument was as transparent as it was chilling: "The earth is merely a temporary way station on the road to eternal life. It is unimportant except as a place of testing to get into heaven. The earth was put here by the Lord for his people to subdue and to use for profitable purposes on the way to the hereafter."

This line of reasoning did not end with the Reagan administration. A former administrator of the U.S. Environmental Protection Agency's office on the environment declared that the re-election of President Bush provided a mandate to relax pollution limits for ozone, to eliminate vehicle tailpipe inspections, to ease pollution standards for cars, to allow corporations to keep certain information about environmental problems secret from the public, and to open the Arctic National Wildlife Refuge to drilling.

To the degree that it reflected the administration's fundamentalist supporters, such an attitude shows Christianity at its very worst and in its most dangerous form. This form of traditional Christianity, however much it may still bring comfort to individuals, shows no concern for the salvation of the planet and is becoming a threat to the future of humankind. Clearly, the two kinds of global catastrophe described above are fundamentally different from each other. That envisaged by the fundamentalists is solely in the hands of God; all that humans can do is to passively accept the salvation being offered by God in the Christian Gospel. The ecological crisis, on the other hand, is the result of human action and only humans can do something positive about it.

GOD HELPS THOSE WHO HELP THEMSELVES

If Christianity is to respond to the challenge contained in the manifesto issued by the ecological scientists, it must put its own house in order. It must first reject completely the ancient expectation of a final Armageddon and the literal return of Jesus Christ. Then it must replace this by an appreciative understanding of the real crisis facing humankind—the ecological crisis—and initiate a positive response to it. How can it do that? An American Catholic priest, Thomas Berry, has said, "we must move beyond a spirituality focused simply on the divine and the human to a spirituality concerned with survival of the natural world in its full splendor, its fertility, and its integral well-being."

In the lectures that follow I shall try to sketch what this new spirituality may entail. It could appropriately be called the Greening of Christianity.

7

BEYOND
"OUR FATHER WHO ART IN HEAVEN"

In 1967, in a now famous article in *Science*, University of California history professor Lynn White wrote, "Christianity in absolute contrast to ancient paganism . . . has . . . insisted that it is God's will that man exploit nature for his proper ends." He was referring, of course, to the biblical story of creation in which God created humankind, blessed them, and said, "Be fruitful and multiply and fill the earth and subdue it; and have dominion over the fish of the sea and over the birds of the air and over every living thing that moves upon the earth."

These words are clearly in conflict with our modern need to stabilize population growth, to husband the earth's natural resources, and to acknowledge the interdependence of all planetary species. Not only is this supposedly divine command no longer appropriate, it is positively dangerous now that we humans have filled the earth to overflowing and find it difficult to stop multiplying further. Furthermore, coming as they do from an ancient cultural context very different from our own, these words no longer command uncritical acceptance. Rather, they warrant moral condemnation in that they give humans unlimited power over all other creatures.

A SHARP INDICTMENT, A FLAWED DEFENSE

And Lynn White went further. "Christianity," he said, "bears a huge burden of guilt for the human attitude that we are superior to nature, contemptuous of it, willing to use it for our slightest whim . . . We shall continue to have a worsening ecological crisis until we reject the Christian axiom that nature has no reason for existence save to serve man."

This is the first instance I know of in which Christianity, far from being simply rebuked for not taking sufficient interest in the growing ecological crisis, is actually accused of being the cause of it. This serious (though to many Christians ridiculous) charge does not come from an atheistic opponent of Christianity. White was in fact a practising Presbyterian, yet he felt it incumbent upon himself to draw attention to the dangers he found inherent in traditional Christianity.

Many theologians, of course, came to the defense of Christianity against White's charges. In a short essay in *Man and Nature*, A. R. Peacocke pointed out that "the exploitative, rapacious, attitude to nature" that White quite rightly condemned was by no means uniformly encouraged in Christian society. Christianity had also produced both a St. Francis and a St. Benedict. Peacocke conceded that nature had been de-sacralized by the Old Testament prophets, but he contended that in the biblical view "man is a trustee, steward and manager for that which is not his own and which is of value for its own sake to God."

To be sure, the Bible does refer to stewardship. We find it mentioned, for example, in the well-known parable of the Talents. But nowhere does the Bible teach that the human relationship to the world of nature is one of stewardship. This sort of Christian teaching, commendable though it is, has emerged only very recently, and in direct response to our growing awareness of the ecological crisis. Thus a number of books written from a Christian perspective now expound the stewardship of the earth's resources as a Christian duty.

But is a call to stewardship sufficient as the Christian response to the ecological crisis? Anne Primavesi, for example, has pointed out that even the idea of stewardship can be exploitative and unecological, for it is commonly the task of stewards to maximise the profits both for themselves and for their employers. Such an approach takes little or no account of the inherent rights or worth of the earth's resources, particularly its livestock. Stewardship, in short, still assumes an anthropocentric attitude towards nature and shows no appreciation of the fact that we humans are ourselves part of nature.

Simply learning to be better stewards, then, is not enough. Christianity must make more radical changes in its understanding of our place and role in nature. In 1973 the celebrated historian Arnold Toynbee put his finger on the problem when he wrote, "Some of the major maladies of the present day world—in particular the recklessly extravagant consumption of nature's irreplaceable treasures, and the pollution of those of them that man has not already devoured—can be traced back to a religious cause, and this cause is the rise of monotheism."

THE ORIGIN OF MONOTHEISM

To understand why Toynbee made such a serious and alarming charge against the monotheistic traditions, we need to understand how monotheism arose. This is no frivolous proviso, for only in very recent times have we been in a position to conceive of what Karen Armstrong has brilliantly outlined in her recent best seller, *A History of God.* Throughout most of Christian history the reality of God as the Creator and controller of the universe appeared to be so self-evidently true that it was not open to question. Only since the time of Darwin has it become clear that all languages, all cultures, and all religions are of human origin. Since the very concept "god" is the creation of human imagination, "the history of God" catalogues the wide variety of ways in which this idea has been understood. It is not a little ironic that the Bible proved to be an important documentary source for writing such a history.

Let me briefly sketch the rise of monotheism. All people of primal societies—take for example the pre-European Maori of New Zealand—saw themselves dependent upon the forces of nature. They personified these forces as unseen gods and spirits who controlled all the changing phenomena of the natural world. These gods must be obeyed if humans were to continue to enjoy the necessities of life provided by them. Chief among the gods were the Sky-Father and the Earth-Mother. The Sky-Father presided over the heavenly bodies, and controlled thunder, lightning, and storms. The Earth-Mother provided for humankind the fruits she produced from her bountiful vegetation.

In our tradition, the beginning of true monotheism is to be found in the Israelite prophets, who over a period of some five hundred years weaned the people of Israel from their dependence upon the gods of nature—first by denying they had any reality and then by replacing them with the one God Yahweh. Henceforth, the prophets declared, the whole of humankind was to worship and obey only Him. This was the very first commandment: "I am Yahweh your God. You shall acknowledge no other gods before me." This God was not only the Creator and the Provider; he was also the Lord of history. Thus came to birth the kind of monotheism that has been the foundation of faith for Jew, Christian, and Muslim ever since.

FROM THE MANY TO THE ONE

This transition from polytheism to monotheism took some centuries and was more complex than the simplistic summary I shall now sketch, but in effect what happened was this. Yahweh, the national god of the Israelites, who delivered them from slavery in Egypt, had originated both as the God of war who led people to victory, and also as the Sky-God who manifested his wrath against misdeeds in storms and droughts. The well-known biblical term, "Lord of hosts" can be translated, both as "God of the armies" and as "God of the stars." It is this Israelite Sky-God, Yahweh, who eventually became transformed into the monotheistic deity of Jew, Christian, and Muslim. That is why we continue to address him, as we do in the Lord's Prayer, with the familiar words "Our Father who art in heaven." In this transition Yahweh became universalized and all other gods were banished from existence.

At the time, this movement from polytheism to monotheism was a great intellectual and spiritual advance. Its replacement of multiplicity with a simple unity provides an interesting example of Ockham's razor, the philosophical principle that simple theories are to be preferred to complex ones. The transition to monotheism had the potential to unify all humankind by means of a common faith. The capacity of monotheism to win universal conviction is shown by the fact that despite its fragmentation into three often antagonistic subdivisions—Jewish Christian, and Islamic—it has lasted more than two and a half thousand years.

MONOTHEISM FLAWED

But as we have only recently begun to recognize, monotheism brought with it several unfortunate corollaries. The first is that

God, having originated as the Sky Father, has always been spoken of in male terms. This has had the effect of nurturing and authorizing patriarchal societies in which women were demeaned. As Mary Daly, the most outspoken exponent of feminist theology so trenchantly said, "Where God is male, the male reigns supreme." Women came to be considered too carnal to perform holy and priestly functions, and lest they deflect males from the path of humble obedience to God, their fleshly charms needed to be hidden. Even such recent theologians as Karl Barth and Dietrich Bonhoeffer were still defending the supremacy of men over women on theological grounds. As the women's liberation movement rightly contended, it has now become necessary to take our cue from the title of Mary Daly's book and move *Beyond God the Father.*

Second, the advent of monotheism annihilated the goddesses of nature so successfully that the Hebrew Bible does not contain a single word meaning "goddess." One or two personal names of ancient Canaanite goddesses have survived; we find Ashtoreth, goddess of fertility, but only after her name had been deliberately disfigured by replacing its vowels with those of the Hebrew word for "shame"—an ancient example of what we might term "theological correctness."

Thus the original gender balance existing in polytheism disappeared in monotheism, and women were left at a spiritual disadvantage since they had no feminine figure or icon to identify with. To fill this spiritual vacuum is probably the reason for the development of the cult of the Virgin Mary in the Christian tradition, and for her acclamation as the Queen of Heaven.

Third, because the Earth-Mother was one of the nature gods to be annihilated, the earth itself became desacralized. All of the sacred power it once possessed was effectively transferred to another world—the heavenly dwelling place of God the Father—and the forces of nature now became impersonal phenomena that God could control by way of reward and punishment. Even worse, Christians came to regard the earth as a fallen world and found evidence of this in the way species preyed on one another, in what but recently was proverbially called "nature red in tooth and claw."

Fourth, monotheism led to the dualistic view of reality that dominated traditional Christianity up until modern times. It helped to deepen the contrast between the earthly and the heavenly, the material and spiritual, the human and the divine, the temporal and the eternal. And thus the natural world, previously venerated as the source of the necessities of life, came to be seen as degraded, under divine judgment, and destined for destruction.

Fifth, monotheism preserved in this one God such personal qualities and virtues as had been found in the gods of nature. Although capable of being angry and vengeful, he came to be seen primarily as all-powerful, all-knowing and all-loving. God was the infinite mind who planned the universe, provided it with its order and wonder, and continued to control its affairs. All the gratitude, fear, and wonder that the original polytheists had felt towards the gods of nature were now to be directed to "Our Father who art in heaven."

DANGEROUS AMBIVALENCES

Humankind's pious worship of the gods of nature had previously held in check its greedy impulse to exploit nature. But the rise of monotheism, as Toynbee observed, "removed this age-old restraint," freed humankind to do what it wished with the natural world, and even encouraged it to exert domination over all living creatures. This is why he declared monotheism to be responsible for the coming ecological crisis.

We should note in passing, however, that the desacralization of the earth did produce some positive results. Most important, it permitted and even fostered the rise of empirical science, for only after the earth had lost its presumed sacred power did the first scientists feel free to experiment with natural phenomena. The German physicist and philosopher Carl Friedrich von Weizsäcker suggested in his 1959 Gifford lectures on *The Relevance of Science* that except for Christian monotheism, modern science would not have evolved as it did. "The concept of strict and generally valid laws of nature could hardly have arisen without the Christian concept of creation. In this sense I call modern science a legacy of Christianity."

The enterprise of empirical science has undoubtedly been of great benefit to humankind, particularly during the nineteenth and twentieth centuries. But lately science itself is beginning to set off alarm bells, first with nuclear weapons and now with genetic modification. We are coming to recognize that our ability to control and even modify nature has become so powerful as to threaten devastating effects on the future. Jürgen Moltmann, one of today's leading German theologians, has said much the same as Toynbee: "It was the Western 'religion of modern times' that freed the way for the secularization of nature. The ancient view about the harmony between the forces of nature has been destroyed—destroyed by modern monotheism on the one hand, and by scientific mechanism on the other. Modern monotheism has robbed nature of its divine mystery and has broken its spell."

A NECESSARY STEP

Because of the ecological crisis now looming, it has become necessary to move beyond monotheism—beyond the idea of "Our Father in heaven, omnipotent creator and controller of the earth." As Jürgen Moltmann explains, "If modern society is to have any future, what we need above all is a new respect for nature, and a new reverence for the life of all created things."

But how can Christianity move beyond monotheism? Does not that belief underlie all Christian teaching? The answer to this question, strangely enough, is "Yes and No!" Yes, because most Christians, including most clergy and theologians still defend monotheism and focus on the heavenly Father as if He alone were God. No, because they too conveniently forget that by the fifth century Christianity had abandoned true monotheism and replaced it with trinitarianism. Indeed, Christianity's innovative modification of the doctrine helped Islam spread as rapidly as it did among Eastern Christians, for in this regard Islam saw itself as a movement commissioned by Allah to restore a pure monotheism.

Christianity's new image of God, the Holy Trinity of Father, Son, and Holy Spirit, was made necessary to do justice to its unique new doctrine of the Incarnation—the declaration that God had enfleshed himself in the man Jesus. This doctrine, which shocked Jews and Muslims into reinforcing their pure monotheism, implied that there no longer exists an impassable gulf between heaven and earth, between the divine and the human, between the supernatural and the natural worlds. The gap has been bridged; God has come down to earth.

The doctrine of the incarnation was the first step in reconnecting the divine Creator with creation, or what we call nature. This radically new departure from strict monotheism would lead at last to the modern secular world. That it should have taken so long should not surprise us. Just as the transition from polytheism to monotheism was a slow and complex process that took some centuries, so the movement beyond monotheism has been gradual and multi-faceted.

The twin doctrines of the Incarnation and of the Holy Trinity proved too revolutionary even for most Christians to cope with, let alone Jews and Muslims. The human Jesus became lost from view behind the wholly divine Christ, who was proclaimed a kind of Hindu-style "avatar" of God the Father. The radical significance of the incarnation was thus obliterated, and the gulf between heaven and earth reappeared. The doctrine of the incarnation had been hijacked by the increasingly dualistic view of reality that dominated the Middle Ages.

NATURE FINDS A VOICE

Yet even in that theologically reactionary climate there arose a brave attempt to reconnect God with the world of nature. St. Francis exhorted Christians to value nature for its own sake. He saluted all earthly creatures as his brothers and sisters, and in the well-known hymn he bequeathed to us he even speaks of "Dear Mother Earth." He founded the order of the Franciscan Friars, from which came Roger Bacon, the man who took the first practical steps towards empirical science. Then followed another Franciscan, William of Ockham, whose philosophy spelled the end of metaphysical speculation and helped to promote the Renaissance, during which humanist scholars and artists affirmed the inherent value and creative potential in the human condition. People began to look with new eyes at the natural world and the universe itself. Artists found beauty and wonder not hitherto experienced in craggy mountains and natural landscapes untouched by humans.

The Renaissance led to the Protestant Reformation, which in turn precipitated the closure of the monastic institutions and forced thousands of nuns and monks out into the secular world. Then came Galileo, whose scientific exploration of the heavens demonstrated that the heavenly bodies were of the same physical order as the earth.

All of these events occurring in fairly rapid succession propelled Western Christianity into a period of accelerating cultural change—one marked by an ever-increasing focus on the physical universe. The inevitable result was the dissolution of the dualistic worldview and its replacement by today's monistic view of the space-time continuum as the only reality. We now commonly refer to this process of cultural change as secularization, seldom recalling that it is the long-term result of the doctrine of the incarnation. Although Christians have been all too slow to realize this, it was acknowledged by the Anglican theologian J. R. Illingworth, who as long ago as 1891 wrote in his essay on the Incarnation, "Secular civilization has co-operated with Christianity to produce the modern world. It is nothing less than the providential correlative and counterpart of the incarnation."

WHAT DOES "GOD" MEAN?

But in this process what has happened to the God of monotheism? What does it mean to speak of God if we go beyond "Our Father who art in heaven"? What is now to be our image of God? Ever more anxiously in the last 400 years the Western world has been wrestling with such questions and propounding a variety of answers. Those who suggested new answers did not receive much help from the church; indeed they often found themselves ostracized, for as a rule the church forbade such questions to be asked.

One proposed answer was that God is to be found everywhere in the world of nature. Known as pantheism, this view was pioneered in the seventeenth century by the Jewish philosopher Spinoza. He began to treat the terms "God" and "Nature" as interchangeable. I doubt whether he realized how close he was to the attitude of the ancient Israelite sages. They had largely ignored the kind of monotheism promoted by the prophets. They did not expect to receive any direct messages from God, nor did they look to God to solve their problems for them. When they spoke of God, as they occasionally did, they used the word as if it were a symbolic name for the way things work in the natural world—perhaps in part because the Hebrew language then had no word meaning "nature."

Even Jesus of Nazareth seems to have been such a sage; what else can one make of his insistence that "God makes his sun rise on the evil and on the good and sends rain on the just and on the unjust"? Thus already in the biblical tradition there is a stream of thought that identifies God with nature—and in such a way as to acknowledge the amoral character of natural forces. The recent disastrous tsunami affords a useful illustration. Pure monotheists felt themselves obliged to interpret this as an act of divine judgment, as the Anglican Dean of Sydney is said to have done. But the Israelite sages would have said, "That is the way that nature operates, and one must learn to respond accordingly." And that was the attitude of Jesus in his famous parable commending the wisdom of the man who in anticipation of storm and flood built his house on a firm foundation.

But the pantheistic answer of equating God with nature has not proved to be wholly satisfactory. For one thing, it soon makes all reference to God redundant and hence leads to atheism. This may be illustrated by the famous reply of the French scientist Laplace to Napoleon. When Laplace presented his astronomical explanation of the movement of the heavenly bodies, Napoleon asked him about the role of God in his theory and Laplace replied, "I have no need of that hypothesis." Here is Ockham's razor with a vengeance: our growing understanding of the way nature works obviates the need to postulate an infinite divine mind controlling its operation. The heavenly bodies, wind and rain, earthquakes and tsunamis operate according to nature's fixed laws, which in turn are quite amoral and completely disinterested with respect to how they affect earthly life.

Pantheism also leaves unanswered other questions that mono-theism appeared to answer: Why is nature here at all? Why is there something and not nothing? To respond to these, the answer known as deism was formulated. It retained sufficient of the monotheistic God to affirm him as the creator of the universe, the first cause, and the designer of the laws of nature. But having set everything in orderly motion, the deists' God played no further active role in the world, either in physics (so miracles did not occur) or in human history (he did not answer prayer or control human events).

The glaring omission in pantheism, atheism, and deism was their lack of any reference to the supreme moral values of justice, com-passion, and love that have long been claimed as attributes of God. How were they to be accounted for?

A DANIEL COME TO JUDGMENT

The first person to bring them into the equation was Ludwig Feuerbach. In 1841 his epoch-making book, *The Essence of Christianity*, shocked contemporary readers by asserting that "God" is a humanly created concept. Although the Bible tells us God made human beings in his image, the truth (said Feuerbach) is that humans have made God in *their* image. Using the psy-chological technique of projection (widely understood today but unknown in Feuerbach's time), he argued that our ancient forbears had unconsciously projected onto this humanly created concept such moral qualities as justice, love, compassion, and forgiveness— which all humans revere and to which they aspire. Thus reassigned, they became greatly magnified and were judged to be the divine attributes. "The personality of God," he said, "is nothing else than the projected personality of man." Today some people find that conclusion almost a truism, while others reject it as fiercely as people did in Feuerbach's day. "God is our highest idea," said Feuerbach; and curiously enough that is how Anselm, 800 years earlier, began his famous "proof" of the existence of God.

What is often overlooked, however, is that Feuerbach's deconstruction of God did not stop there. First he showed that the very essence of Christianity was its doctrine of the incarnation. Making the human Jesus the new basis of religion and treating him as divine meant that the heavenly throne was now empty. As Paul said, Jesus Christ represented the new humanity that had to accept responsibility for functions and goals previously projected on to the Father in heaven.

Unfortunately, Feuerbach's subsequent book, *The Essence of Religion*, never received the public attention of the first one. In it he pointed out that since his first book had dealt only with the moral and personal attributes of God, more remained to be said. When viewed as the creator and controller of the natural world, God had taken over the functions of the earlier gods of nature; accordingly, the monotheistic image of God also embodied what Feuerbach called the "personified essence of nature."

It is important to see what Feuerbach had thus done. He had deconstructed the God concept into two quite different orders of reality: the world of nature (as emphasized by the pantheists and deists) and the collection of supreme human values (as emphasized by the theists). As Feuerbach saw it, God was the projection of both the essence of nature and the essence of humanity—and therefore the monotheistic God had long served as the way to understand both the natural world and the human condition.

THE RESOLUTION OF THEOLOGY INTO TWO AREAS

Now if theology means the study of God, then Feuerbach's deconstruction of God has effectively resolved theology into two complementary areas—the study of nature on the one hand, and the study of humanity and its values on the other. An interesting way of illustrating this is to observe what has happened to Western institutions of higher learning in the last 800 years. At the time they were founded it was thought that all knowledge could be understood as a manageable unity: hence the name "university." But the medieval university was based on, and revolved around, the Faculty of Theology, the discipline then known as the Queen of the Sciences.

Perhaps the last person to attempt to expound all knowledge as a unity was Thomas Aquinas, who set out to reconcile Aristotle's philosophy of nature with what was assumed to be the truth received by divine revelation. This he did in his renowned *Summa Theologica*, which he did not live to finish. But his synthesis was never universally accepted, and eventually it broke down, opening the way for the explosion of academic disciplines in modern times.

They fall into two main groups: the physical sciences study the natural world, while the social sciences and the arts study humanity and culture. These two groups have now replaced the theology faculty that by itself sufficed in the twelfth century, when simple monotheism was universally accepted. What is more, by the middle of the twentieth century there was such an evident rift between these two groups that the scientist C. P. Snow wrote some widely read novels deploring what he judged to be the bifurcation of society into "two cultures" that no longer understood each other. By the end of the century, however, this rift was being partially healed by a growing mutual respect among scholars of different fields. Let us look briefly in turn at these two areas, which both began as provinces of theology.

I was thinking of that foundational discipline when I said earlier that this series could well have been entitled "From theo-logy to eco-logy." I meant that we have moved far beyond focusing our attention on an unseen personal God who designed and controls the world in which we live. We now focus our attention on the physical universe itself. This we have found to be almost infinite in space and time and to operate according to its own internal laws. And even though our mind's eye catches occasional glimpses of a greater dimension, we acknowledge ourselves to be a part of the natural world—physical organisms who live and die like all the simpler forms of life in this complex web we call the ecosphere. If we are to live life to its full potential, we need to understand the ecosphere and respond to it appropriately.

One of the most important lessons we learn from ecology is that the forces of nature do not operate according to any moral plan or ultimate purpose. Rather, nature operates according to what Jacques Monod has called a process of "chance and necessity." Unlike monotheism, ecology leaves us with no assurance that we live in a moral world where everything will work out for the best in the end. Since nature shows no special interest in the human race, when we move beyond monotheism we have no divine deliverer to turn to. Rather, we must now treat the forces of nature with the respect they deserve; for our life and well-being depend on them, and we know not when or how they may bring life to an end. (Witness the sudden end of the age of dinosaurs!) Such a view of nature, incidentally, is not wholly foreign to the biblical tradition. We find it, as we have seen, in the sages. More than two thousand years ago Ecclesiastes observed that we humans are all subject to "time and chance."

OUR SEARCH FOR VALUE AND MEANING

Now let us turn to the second branch of learning, that concerned with human culture and values—and the one to which traditional academic theology retreated. When our ancient ancestors began to ask basic questions about human existence, their answers became the world's many cultures and religions. This why the concept of God came more and more to embody our highest values and to satisfy our search for meaning and purpose. And though the concept of God has been deconstructed and can no longer be taken to be the name of a thinking and acting supernatural being, the term "God" may still remain useful as both the symbolic embodiment of our desire to find meaning in life and the metaphoric equivalent of such values as love, justice, truth, and compassion, which continue to lay powerful claims upon us.

The theologian Gordon Kaufman, for example, thinks we need this traditional word "God" if only as a symbol, because it provides us with "an ultimate point of reference" and thereby enables us to unify and order our experience of reality in the mental world we construct for ourselves. The image of God that remains, therefore, is the sum total of the very values once described as his attributes. God is the symbolic name for the aggregate of our highest values.

This process had begun by New Testament times, for that text already affirms that "God is love." In modern times the symbolization has gone much further. Mahatma Gandhi, for example, said that "God is truth." Leo Tolstoy (in *War and Peace*) says, "Life is God and to love life is to love God." Don Cupitt, in making a study of how our daily language is changing, found a large collection of phrases now coming into common usage that include the term "life." "How's life treating you?" "That's what life is all about!" "I need to move on in life." "Get a life!" It is as if in daily secular speech we are now unconsciously turning to the word "life" as the natural replacement for the once common term "God."

Gordon Kaufman's book *In Face of Mystery* comes to this conclusion: "To believe in God is to commit oneself to a particular way of ordering one's life and action. It is to devote oneself to working towards a fully humane world within the ecological restraints here on planet Earth, while standing in piety and awe before the profound mysteries of existence."

Clearly, the Greening of Christianity stands in strong contrast to much of the historical tradition. In the latter we humans saw ourselves as helpless creatures, passively dependent on the grace and power of an external supernatural being. In Green Christianity we find that the responsibility for our future and that of the ecosphere has been placed upon us. By our chosen actions we must enflesh the values we once regarded as the attributes of God. That is what the incarnation means. We are required to be perfect in the way God symbolized perfection. Of course, as you no doubt recognize, I am simply quoting what Jesus the sage said in the Sermon on the Mount.

Are we really up to that? The impending ecological crisis gives us no option but to try. In the next lecture we shall explore what that attempt will entail.

8

THE ECOLOGICAL IMPERATIVE, A NEW ETHICAL DIMENSION

When I was a theological student, one of the chief textbooks on Christian Ethics was *The Divine Imperative*, written by the celebrated Swiss theologian Emil Brunner. This 700–page tome, published in English in 1937, is not only laborious to study but strikes today's reader as rather odd. It discussed divorce and contraception, but never once mentioned homosexuality—a topic that in our time so divides Christians. Written in the aftermath of World War I, it declared war to have outlived its purpose, but made no reference to peacemaking. These points strikingly exemplify how much our ethical problems have changed in seventy years. I refer to the book because for this lecture I have half borrowed its title by way of recalling that Christian ethics was long assumed to be an exposition of the human behavior that God has commanded—hence *The Divine Imperative*.

But the disintegration of monotheism that was outlined in the last lecture means that ethics can no longer be based on divine commandments supposedly revealed in the distant past. Some have interpreted this to mean we are now free to do whatever we like. Nietzsche thought the death of God would cause the collapse of the whole system of Christian thought. Dostoevsky complained that the absence of God meant that everything is permissible. Not so!

A NEW DISPENSATION

As long ago as the end of the Enlightenment, the great modern philosopher Immanuel Kant (1724–1804) had shifted the base of ethics from divine revelation to what he called "the moral law within." He was referring to the experience of a sense of moral duty, and called it "the categorical imperative." Of course, this radical shift has made ethical decision-making a great deal more difficult than it used to be. It is no longer simply a matter of debating how to interpret a divine commandment. Now we must first decide why it is that some actions are to be judged right and others wrong. This has led to what is known as "Situation Ethics," a process by which one must examine all the factors in the situation that impinge on the ethical dilemma, and then decide which course of action will promote the maximum well-being for all concerned.

The global crisis outlined in the first lecture is alerting us to the radically new situation in which the human race finds itself, one that calls for making ethical decisions of a kind it has never had to face before. Unfortunately, we are ill prepared for this task, partly because our Christian past has left us unskilled in the new mode of ethical decision-making, and partly because too few are even aware of the critical situation in which we now live.

To contrast this new situation with the old, we need only recall that until 200 years ago the whole of the Western world lived by the story of human origins as told by the Bible. Nearly everyone accepted as fundamental to ethics the idea that the earth and all within it was created by God, who still holds it in his control; that He made us to be like him and, to guide us, he revealed his Divine will; and that since this has been permanently recorded in Holy Writ, our duty is simply to obey. It is by this formula that traditional Christianity still struggles to decide such contemporary issues as birth control, homosexual behavior, and the ordination of women.

But for all reasonably well-informed and thoughtful people, the biblical story of origins has now been replaced by an entirely new story; and this scenario sketches the changing universe from the "big bang" onwards, through the evolution of life on this planet, followed more recently by the evolution of human culture. The new story of origins not only leaves us with an entirely different picture of the vast universe we live in, but describes our relationship with the earth in strikingly different terms.

READING FROM A NEW PAGE

This modern understanding of the source of our being indicates that while we rightly value what we may call the spiritual dimension of the human condition, no absolute gulf exists between us and the other living creatures. As Teilhard de Chardin so wonderfully put it, all physical matter has the potential for spirituality. Therefore, the spiritual dimension of human experience can never be divorced from the physical, and the supposed dichotomy between spiritual and material is spurious. We humans are psycho-physical organisms. We must abandon the widespread but false notion that we are spiritual beings only temporarily encased in physical bodies—a notion that derives, after all, not from the Bible but from the Greek philosopher Plato.

Furthermore, the new story of origins returns us humans to our proper place among the many and diverse life forms on this planet. As the American Catholic priest Thomas Berry has said, everything on earth is cousin to everything else. This has now been scientifically demonstrated by the genetic code, the mechanism that determines the physiological structure of every creature and that shows how we are related to all other forms of planetary life. We humans have no special rights of ownership and dominion over the others.

Our problem, says Berry, is that we are living between the two stories. While we are still trying to accept the implications of the new story, much that belonged to the old story still lingers on in our thinking—even though it has become not only obsolete, but positively dysfunctional.

"I SET BEFORE YOU TODAY FACT AND FICTION . . ."

In the old story we were subject to the dictates of the Heavenly Father, and believed ourselves to have been given dominion over the earth. In the new story we have lost our privileged place in the web of planetary life, and find ourselves subject to the same forces of nature as are all other living organisms.

In the old story storms, droughts, and earthquakes were "acts of God" and were thought to have moral significance. In the new story the forces of nature have no personal interest in us at all. Yet although totally amoral, they can determine whether we live or die, and we ignore them at our peril.

These forces constitute the parameters within which all planetary life has evolved. Humans have evolved within limits set by the earth's conditions. Our physique, for example, is suited to the mass of the planet earth; we could not survive on a planet with Jupiter's gravity. Fascinating though it may be to imagine future space travel to distant stars, it will almost certainly be never more than a delightful fantasy. We are earth creatures, who can live only within the delicately balanced natural forces, geographical conditions, and interdependence of species that constitute the ecology of our planetary home. Because of our new understanding of our origins and of the nature of our ecological home, the ethic that concerns us today is no longer the divine imperative but what may be called the Ecological Imperative.

But no one should conclude that the shift from the divine imperative to the ecological imperative represents an ominous new heresy, for it involves not rejection, but reorientation. "The Greening of Christianity" means that Christian thinking must now incorporate all that we have learned about the human species from the human sciences—including, of course, the relatively new science of anthropology. (Few today are aware that "anthropology" originated as a theological term; it referred to the Christian doctrine of the human condition.) In the last two hundred years our understanding of the human species and of its relationship to the natural world has changed so drastically that, as Feuerbach showed, theology has been turned upside down—or more appropriately, inside out.

COMMON GROUND

That being the case, one might expect the ecological imperative to have little or nothing in common with the earlier Christian doctrine of humankind. Surprisingly, this is not so. The biblical myth of origins declared with striking boldness that we humans are formed of the dust of the ground, and when our lives come to an end we return to dust. Three thousand years later we still use the words of that ancient story at our funeral services—"earth to earth, ashes to ashes, dust to dust." The biblical proposition that we are made of earth remains basically unchallenged, though of course we are now more sophisticated and know that the "dust" we are made of consists chiefly of atoms of carbon, hydrogen, nitrogen, and oxygen. And whereas the biblical myth pictured God forming us much as a child makes mudpies, we are now aware of the complex nature of human physiology. The lifeless atoms of which we are composed are united in the most intricate designs to form the myriads of living cells and the many internal organs that constitute the human organism.

But common ground with the ancient myth does not stop there. We are becoming increasingly aware of how fundamentally our amazing internal systems depend upon an appropriate environment. And in its quaint but profound way, the biblical myth acknowledges this new ecological insight as well. After the fashioning of the human body from dust, says the Bible, God breathed his breath into it. Since Hebrew uses the same word to mean breath, spirit, wind, and air, we can translate the ancient myth into modern terminology by saying that though we humans are made of the same elements as are found in the ground beneath our feet, we come alive and stay alive only if we supported by the correct atmosphere. Indeed, we cannot live more than about two minutes without breathing it.

What in ancient times was understood simply as our dependence on the breath of God has in modern times become expanded into the highly sophisticated study of ecology. The ecosphere has now become, to use Paul's quoted phrase, the God "in whom we live and move and have our being." In 1993 Sallie McFague wrote *The Body of* God, in which she proposed an ecological theology centered on this striking new image: "The body of God is not *a* body but all the different, peculiar, particular bodies about us." She called this an incarnational theology, for it points out that what our forbears understood and treated as the divine is now to be found all around us and within us in the ecosphere. This being so, we must respect every "body," animate and inanimate, in the natural world—and value it for its own sake and not as a means to an end. We are immediately reminded of words attributed to Jesus: "Whatever you do for the least of these my brothers, you do for me."

Thus worship directed to the Heavenly Father is to be replaced by our grateful acknowledgment of the ecosphere's all-surpassing worth to us, and dutiful obedience to the God of heaven must be changed to devotion to the ecological imperative of doing what the ecosphere requires of us. Even the doctrine of sin, so prominent in traditional Christianity, has its new counterpart. The belief that Adam's disobedience condemned all humans to a tragic state of alienation from the God is superseded by our alarming awareness that humanity is currently at war with the very planet that has given it birth and sustenance.

TAKE A BREATH . . .

To discuss the ecological imperative further, let us start with the atmosphere, for it is the most critical parameter set by the ecosphere for planetary creatures. From time immemorial our ancestors simply took the atmosphere for granted. It is only in recent times that we have been forced to recognize how dependent we are upon it and how we have evolved to fit its particular gaseous mixture—one that consists chiefly of nitrogen and oxygen and has been stable for some millions of years. If we travel to the moon we must take our supply with us. Even climbing high mountains often requires extra supplies of oxygen. Every time we board a plane we are solemnly reminded by the cabin attendant how to use the oxygen supply in an emergency.

Some gases, even in small quantities, are highly toxic to us. One of these is carbon monoxide; yet since the introduction of the internal combustion engine we have been releasing this substance into the atmosphere in ever greater quantities. The air in some heavily populated cities is now so polluted as to be unhealthy, and in some cases positively dangerous. One of the most basic ecological imperatives, then, is to control every practice that pollutes our most basic requirement for life and thus to keep the composition of the atmosphere stable.

This task points to the mysterious and wonderful character of the earth's ecology. We humans, along with all other breathing creatures on the planet, have for millions of years been unknowingly cooperating with the vegetation in keeping the right balance of the gases in the atmosphere. We breathe in oxygen and breathe out carbon dioxide. Plants and trees absorb carbon dioxide and release oxygen. This balancing act, which has long kept the composition of the atmosphere stable, is only one of many of the earth's phenomena which led the scientist James Lovelock to liken the earth itself to an organism whose living skin is the biosphere in the same way as bark is the living skin of the tree. For this reason he referred to the earth as Gaia, reviving the name for Mother Earth found in ancient Greek mythology.

. . . AND BE INSPIRED

Of course Lovelock did not mean that the earth is a thinking, planning being, but that it has many characteristics of a living system. The earth's outer layer is made up of all forms of life from the viruses to the great whales and from tiny ocean algae to the giant redwoods, all living within their own special ecosystems and yet integrated with the atmosphere, the ocean, and the surface rocks and soils. But all of these have evolved in such a complex network of delicate balances with one another that the earth appears to have fashioned for itself an all encompassing and self-regulatory system. Just as our own bodies have immune systems that protect us from disease and thermostats to keep us at a constant temperature, so the earth seems to regulate itself, keeping the climate constant and comfortable, and preserving just the right amount of oxygen in the air and the right amount of salt in the oceans.

When we humans upset these balances—say by increasing the carbon dioxide in the atmosphere—we are attacking the earth's regulatory system in a manner analogous to the way AIDS ravages an individual. But as participants in this amazing ecosphere, we are obliged by the ecological imperative to understand it, respect it, and take appropriate actions to nurture it and preserve all its balances.

The earth has been a living, evolving system for some three and a half billion years. We humans are very late comers on the scene. If we threaten the ecosphere too severely, it will eliminate us from its system—though no more by conscious decision than does one's personal immune system eliminate invading bacteria. Just as individuals can cause their own death by foolishly defying the law of gravity, so the human species can effect its own extinction along with that of many other species by willful and thoughtless interference with the ecological conditions on which our survival depends.

Our growing knowledge of how life has evolved, and of the earthly parameters within which all creatures live, has amounted to a new revelation that supplements and largely replaces the supposed revelations of the past. Unfortunately, those who focus their attention too closely on the divine epiphanies of the past tend to be blind to present secular manifestations. That is why, as we noted in the first of this series of lectures, it has been left largely to prophets outside of the churches to read the signs of the times in our day.

This should not surprise us. The periods of new growth and development in the Judeo-Christian tradition have always started on the margins rather than at the center of the tradition. Jesus himself was neither a priest nor one schooled in the rabbinic academies, but a wandering sage. Similarly, the first to become aware of the new revelations, and to become the pioneers of the modern secular world, lived on the fringes of Christian society rather than at its center.

SECULAR PROPHETS

These prophets from the secular branches of Western culture are now loudly proclaiming the ecological imperative through books, lectures and protests. They are calling us all to be active in stabilizing population, in halting our wasteful and destructive ways, in avoiding pollution of air and water, in conserving the earth's non-renewable resources, and in changing to renewable sources of energy. The good news is that these ecological imperatives are being adopted by many individuals and voluntary groups, as well as by local, national, and international forms of government; conservation and environmentalism are now being acknowledged as highly desirable social aims.

Thomas Berry welcomes these moves as the beginning of a vast sea change in human consciousness, one that will take us forward to a new understanding of what it means to be human. He believes that such a radical re-evaluation of life and the resulting new sense of values will not only lead us out of our self-centered worlds, but even come to transcend our national loyalties. We may call it the rise of *green consciousness.*

It is manifesting itself world wide in a great variety of ways. At both national and international levels, ministries and commissions are now devoted to the care of the environment. Numerous major international conferences have been convened, and such new organizations as Greenpeace and the Bird and Forest Society have been founded. We also see the emergence of many one-issue movements, positive responses that have ironically revived some of our most basic religious words. We hear"salvation" echoed in slogans like "Save Manapouri"; "Save the black robin"; "Save the blue-eyed penguin." "Sanctuary" is another religious term to return in secular garb. It once referred to holy places where the divine presence was thought to offer protection to the weak and vulnerable; now when we set out to save endangered fauna, we establish "bird sanctuaries," "fish sanctuaries," or "wild life sanctuaries."

Once again these point to the earthy, fleshly nature of the Christian doctrine of the incarnation. The more that Christianity's belief and practice came to emphasize the saving of souls, the more it lost sight of its most unique and central doctrine.

For the same reason Christians long held themselves aloof from the earthy world of politics, yet it was inevitable that green consciousness would find political expression. New Zealand can justifiably claim to have been one of the first countries to see the rise of such a political party. In the 70's it was called the Values Party. Since that time Green Parties have been springing up throughout the Western world, seeking to bring green consciousness to bear on all government decisions.

A WIDER HORIZON

But the ecological imperative calls for doing more than even governments have the power to achieve. Multi-national corporate bodies, for example, are not only beyond the control of any one national government, but often influence national policy. Unfortunately, they tend to dismiss green consciousness as a passing fad, based on false evidence, and dangerously alarmist. Their resistance to environmental issues is quite understandable because it is built into the economic principles underlying capitalism itself, principles that since the fall of communism in Eastern Europe have been widely adopted around the globe.

A primary axiom of capitalism is that a nation's well-being depends upon the wealth produced by its industry, technology, and economic development, the aggregate of which can be measured by its per capita Gross National Product (GNP). The natural corollary is that to achieve maximum well-being a nation must maximize its economic growth. Thus annual economic growth is commonly being used as a criterion to measure the success or failure of political policies. Modern economic orthodoxy regards these precepts to be not only basic to capitalism but also normative for the way humans relate to the natural world.

But will western-style capitalism respond to the ecological imperative? Some are already prophesying quite the contrary, fearing that capitalism is leading the world to the edge of an abyss because its fundamental principles are ultimately destructive of the ecology of the earth. In 1989 Herman Daly published *For the Common Good: Redirecting the Economy toward Community, the Environment and a Sustainable Future.* In writing this book, the former economist with the World Bank collaborated with theologian John Cobb, well known in the theological world as an exponent of process theology—a system that moved beyond the concept of God as heavenly Father to find the divine reality in the process of evolution itself. These two argued that the standard system of profit-and-loss accounting used by economists is deeply flawed. For example, many solar-powered energy systems seem uneconomical when compared with those dependent on coal, oil or uranium; but when the full cost—including production, consumption of a non-renewable resource, waste disposal, and damage to environment—is taken into account, they could prove to be relatively inexpensive.

Similarly, they argue, the accounting system used for the calculation of GNP can produce seriously misleading results. However useful GNP may be for short-term planning, it gives false expectations about the long term. The trouble is, such a calculation regards a national economy as a self-contained system that can be divorced from its surroundings, whereas in reality it should be treated as a sub-system of the larger ecosystem on which it is dependent. Since all economic activity draws upon raw materials (some of which are irreplaceable), produces waste products (which have to be deposited somewhere), and may well cause damage to the ecosystem (which keeps us alive!), any calculation of GNP that ignores the negative impact caused by these other factors is false. When these subtractions are made, what seemed positive economic growth may well turn out to be in fact negative.

USING 'REAL' NUMBERS

Daly and Cobb argued that producing a balanced picture of the current state of human well-being on the planet requires an assessment in terms of the whole eco-system, not just one of its sub-systems. They set about constructing an alternative benchmark for economic growth, one that took account of the whole system, and called it the Index of Sustainable Economic Welfare (ISEW). Then they applied it to the American economy. Judged by the standard GNP statistics, the U. S. per capita income had increased in real value by 25 per cent since 1976; but the ISEW indicated that over the same period the economic well-being of Americans had actually declined by 10 per cent.

Thus, widespread as green consciousness has now become, it is far from certain that political endeavor and planning at national and international levels is going to achieve the necessary outcomes. The Kyoto protocols have not been adopted by some of the most powerful nations. Even here in New Zealand there is much resistance to carbon taxes. We face the question of how far green consciousness can, or should be, promoted by coercion. China, for instance, has employed drastic measures to deal with the population explosion, restricting each couple to a single child. But elsewhere such heavy-handed legislation is likely to be flatly rejected as totalitarian. Does this mean that the limited power of democratic governments may not be sufficient to arrest the ecological crisis? What is needed is a groundswell of green consciousness at the grassroots of society. What can provide the motivation for that?

<h3 align="center">MOTIVES AND MOTIFS</h3>

Motivation is normally heightened by appeal to self-interest. But is not self-interest at the root of our current problems? Of course it is! Self-interest, however, comes in different kinds. We need to distinguish between individual self-interest and corporate self-interest. The latter has for eons provided the strength of family and tribal units, in which individuals frequently sacrifice their personal interests for the sake of the group. Where group self-interest reigns, the good name of the family and the survival of the tribe take precedence over the desires of the individual.

Unfortunately, such beneficial group cohesion often led to long histories of inter-tribal strife and inter-ethnic war that must now be superseded by global unity. But we are ill prepared for this; tribalism at the national level is still very powerful and is preventing us from meeting the ecological crisis. As individual self-interest gave way to tribal self-interest, so tribal self-interest must now give way to ecological self-interest. We all have a basic interest in preserving the ecology of the planet, both for ourselves and for our descendants. The whole of humanity must pull together.

Christianity likewise began as a movement aimed at uniting all humans in one body, the body of Christ, with "neither Jew nor Gentile, neither freeman nor slave, neither male nor female." After the fall of Rome, Christianity even began to exhibit something of the Empire's *Pax Romana*, but it gradually lost this vision of a united humanity as it became increasingly focused on a spiritual life after death. From that time onwards, corporate self-interest waned, and individual self-interest reasserted itself as people were urged to embrace Christianity in order to be saved from Hell and guaranteed a place in heaven. By offering to save people's souls for life in another world, Christianity lost its own soul in this world, and thus merited the dismissive words of the cynic who said, "the church has become so heavenly-minded as to be of no earthly use."

The hope of personal immortality in a world beyond this one goes back only to the second and third centuries. It developed at a time when Christianity was competing with and being influenced by various salvation cults and other mystery religions. This belief must now be judged an aberration—a concession to personal self-centeredness. To provide motivation for green consciousness, Christianity must rediscover its real roots.

A NEW AND BETTER HOPE

Already in Old Testament times our spiritual forbears were learning to accept their mortality. This was a great spiritual advance, for in the ancient pagan world some sort of belief in an after-life was almost universal. In contrast, the Israelite sages urged their people "to number their days that they might apply their hearts to wisdom." Any intimations of immortality were to be seen in their children and what was bequeathed to them and to society generally. That this acceptance of mortality continued in the early church is evident in the earliest Christian epitaph: *Requiescat In Pace*, "May he/she rest in peace." In the grave one would sleep quietly until the end of time, when all would be raised for the mythical Last Judgment.

This earliest form of Christian belief is our clue to the kind of immortality that is still to be prized most highly. It is not the immortality of the individual, but of the species. It is the species and not the individual that has the capacity to live on from generation to generation. And it is further true of all living species that they are dependent on one another and the earth itself. This is the kind of immortality that ecology is concerned with. Ecological immortality calls for a much greater degree of selflessness than we find in the traditional Christian concept of immortality—a self-serving hope that by a tragic irony became the very opposite of the Christian definition of love found in the Fourth Gospel: "No one has greater love than this, to lay down one's life for one's friends."

Immortality, then, is a quality that pertains to the species rather than to the individual, and above all to the evolving web of life on this planet. We human individuals remain as mortal as all earthly creatures. It is our great privilege even to have been born into this awe-inspiring web of life and to have inherited the evolving human culture created by our forbears. And it is our responsibility to transmit this rich culture to our descendants and to hand on to them the earth itself in the best possible state. That is our only proper role and destiny. This is the ecological version of loving God with all one's heart and of loving one's neighbor as oneself. We must respond to the ecological imperative not primarily for our own personal benefit, but for that of our children, our grandchildren, and countless generations beyond.

Now that I have sketched some of the radical changes in Christian belief and moral behavior that ecology requires, we must finally turn to a consideration of what rites and festivals will be most appropriate to foster and celebrate Green Christianity.

9

GREENING RITES
AND FESTIVALS

In 1976 Arnold Toynbee published his last book, entitled *Mankind and Mother Earth.* "We now stand at a turning-point in the history of the biosphere," he wrote, "It looks as if man will not be able to save himself from the nemesis of his demonic material power and greed unless he allows himself to undergo a change of heart."

But such a revolutionary change of heart, Toynbee warned, would require the kind of motivation usually generated only by religion. Of course he was not looking for a religious revival of the traditional, supernaturalist variety. Rather, he regarded religion as the "human being's necessary response to the mysteriousness of the phenomena that he encounters." Indeed, that is how all religion began.

RETURNING TO ORIGINS

But how will such a spirituality arise in this global, secular age, and whence will it come? No religion has ever been invented from scratch; all have evolved out of whatever preceded them. Thus any future religion will arise out of the faiths of the past—and not only from Christianity, Islam and the like, but also from the pre-Axial nature religions that preceded them. Just as the Protestant Reformers who set out to reform the church went back to what they took to be primitive Christianity, so we now need to go back even further—to the pre-Axial religions.

In doing so we find, perhaps to our surprise, that they have never been wholly eliminated. Underneath the surface of the various layers of Christianity lurk the remnants of religion that focused on nature. For example, tucked away in an obscure corner of many a European cathedral is the sculptured representation of the little green man who symbolised the spirit of nature. And more obviously, we still name the days of the week after the ancient Germanic gods—Sunday for the sun-god, Monday for the moon-god, Wednesday for Woden, and Saturday for Saturn.

These relics remain in spite of the efforts of priests to eliminate everything that smacked of superstitious paganism. The devotees of monotheism were so anxious to reject the gods of nature that they disconnected the human species from the world of nature and focused attention on the human species itself. "Much of our trouble," said the Catholic priest Thomas Berry, "has been caused by our limited modes of thought. We centered ourselves on the individual, on personal aggrandizement. . . . A sense of the planet Earth never entered into our minds."

Christianity taught us to fix our attention on heaven above, and to regard this earth as a fallen world, doomed for ultimate destruction. That is why in medieval times so many withdrew from the world into monasteries and nunneries to prepare themselves spiritually for their ultimate salvation. Even when Protestantism closed the monasteries and took a giant step towards the secularizing of Christianity, they still saw the world as the place where the Devil beguiled and entrapped the careless and the unsuspecting. This conviction, still clearly manifested today, explains why fundamentalism regards those who call for the greening of Christianity as doing the work of the Devil.

TO DOMINATE NATURE OR LOVE IT?

Even theologians of the caliber of Emil Brunner warned against giving too much attention to the world of nature. "Because man has been created in the image of God," he wrote, "therefore he may and should make the earth subject to himself, and should have dominion over all other creatures . . . Man is only capable of realizing his divine destiny when he rises above Nature."

It is not surprising, therefore, that it has been left chiefly to secular prophets and voices outside of the church to take the lead in re-valuing the earth and teaching us how to care for it. Just as two thousand years ago Paul claimed that "God has chosen the foolish in the world to shame the wise," so today one can reasonably assert that Mother Earth now relies on the lefties, Greenies, and despised heretics to shame the leaders of political and religious officialdom.

The very first greenie, as we have already noted, was the man now honored as St. Francis, who pioneered the greening of Christianity back in the thirteenth century. Of course his references to nature were still enfolded within the context of giving honor to the Heavenly Father. We are now free, as he was not, to give our full attention to the immense universe itself, to the mystery of life, and to our dependence on the forces of nature. This is just what theologians such as Gordon Kaufman and Sallie McFague have set out to do. In 1997 McFague wrote *Super, Natural Christians: How we should love nature*, in which she effectively reconnects the Christian tradition with the natural world. And it is noteworthy that female scholars like Rosemary Radford Ruether, Karen Armstrong, and Anne Primavesi have been in the forefront of attempts to expound and popularize a green theology.

STEP BACK TO LEAP AHEAD

Perhaps there is no better way to reconnect Christianity with the natural world than to examine the major Christian festivals and trace them back to their origins in nature. All festivals were origi nally related to the movements of the heavenly bodies, for these were once worshipped as deities. Notice how the monotheists who composed the opening chapter of the Bible deliberately downgraded the sun and the moon—first by declaring them to be created, and second, by stating that their creation did not occur until the fourth day! That three days should pass before it appeared was a real put-down for the sun!

The waxing and waning of the moon and the changing path of the sun divide the passing of time into days, months and years, and thereby determined the time frame for all religious celebrations. But the sun and moon remain just as much time-markers for us as they were for primitive humankind. Indeed, our very bodies have biological clocks built into them and these we have tended to ignore for too long. The daily, monthly, and annual festivals keep us in tune with the rhythms of the earth and may well play an important role in promoting our physical and mental health. The attempt by some health programs and New Age cults to focus on these rhythms is not so outlandish as it may at first appear.

The oldest festivals we know of are those that celebrated the New Year and the appearance of the New Moon. In the biblical tradition the festival the New Moon was particularly important, and we hear much of it in the Old Testament. The prophets saw it as a relic of nature worship and tried to stamp it out. Isaiah vigorously declared that God hated Israel's new moon festivals and found them a wearisome burden.

It is interesting to find that these celebrations had lasted until Isaiah's time, for their origin goes back to the Hebrew patriarchs, who lived a semi-nomadic life. The moon not only provided the light for night travel through the desert but it always seemed more kindly than the sun, whose burning heat could be oppressive. It was much the same for the later people of Arabia, and this explains why the month has remained the dominant segment of time in Islam. The Islamic world has never adopted the solar year, and to this day lives by a twelve-month lunar year that is eleven days shorter than the solar year.

The fact that the lunar and solar cycles do not neatly fit each other has long been a problem for cultures that follow a lunar calendar. We have solved the problem simply by dividing the solar year into twelve months of unequal numbers of days, thus disengaging our months from the actual lunar cycles. The people of ancient Israel solved the problem differently, in a way that has remained Jewish practice to this day. They observed a year of twelve lunar months as does Islam, but unlike Islam they adopted the Babylonian system of introducing a thirteenth month nearly every third year in order to realign their lunar system with the true solar year.

THE CANAANITE CALENDAR

The ancient Hebrews first had to come to terms with the solar year when they entered Canaan, for in becoming one people with the Canaanites they had to accommodate themselves to a predominantly agricultural culture that was closely tied to the solar year. While adopting the seasonal pattern based on the sun, the Israelites continued, as the many biblical references to new moon festivals show, to observe the lunar cycles.

The Canaanites appear to have developed a very complex calendar that divided the year into seven periods of fifty days, a scheme now known as the pentecontad calendar. Each pentecontad consisted of seven times seven days plus one. The number seven was treated as sacred, partly because of the four (approximately) seven-day phases of the Moon and partly because there were seven moving heavenly bodies—the five planets, the sun, and the moon. The seven pentecontads followed New Year's Day, with seven-day interludes after the fourth and the seventh to permit celebration of the Feast of Booths and the Feast of Unleavened bread, respectively. I mention the Pentecontad calendar only because remnants of it have survived to this day in the seven-day week, in the fifty-day period between Easter and Pentecost, and in the Year of Jubilee, or Fiftieth year.

Also surviving from ancient Canaanite practice, but in later forms, were the agricultural festivals: the festival of unleavened bread at the spring equinox, the first fruits (fifty days later) and the ingathering of harvest in the autumn. The Israelites gradually disengaged these festivals from their original connection with nature and turned them into commemorations of basic events in their cultural history. Unleavened bread became the Passover, celebrating the deliverance from Egypt. First fruits became Pentecost, celebrating the giving of the Mosaic Law at Sinai. The ingathering retained the name Booths (or tents), but came to celebrate the long trek through the wilderness.

As Christianity emerged out of Judaism, it transformed the first two of these into Christian festivals. Because Jesus had been crucified during the Passover season, this erstwhile spring festival became the commemoration of the death and resurrection of Jesus Christ. The Jewish Pentecost (originally the festival of first fruits) was similarly taken to signal the coming of the Holy Spirit. In the course of time the Easter celebrations became the most important of all Christian festivals, with Good Friday the holiest day of the year and Easter Sunday the most joyous.

THE MORE IT CHANGES . . .

We too often forget that the Easter festival never entirely shed the practices that betray its connection with the spring festival, whether in Canaan or Europe. In Western Christianity, for example, we still call it Easter, preserving the name of the pagan goddess of spring, *Eostre*. What is more, and often to the chagrin of Christian clergy, its most popular symbols in this secular age are Easter eggs and Easter bunnies—echoes from time immemorial of spring festivals that long preceded the Jewish Passover and the Christian celebration of the death and resurrection of Jesus.

If we wish to reconnect Christianity with nature and foster the kind of religion Toynbee called for, there is perhaps no better way than to return to the origins of our major festivals, all rooted as they were in the celebration of nature. The ecological spirituality of the future will celebrate the wonder of the universe and the mystery of life. It will focus on the natural processes that produced and continue to sustain life. It will encourage people to be grateful for the richness and the beauty of the natural world and to respond positively to the ecological imperative laid upon us all.

Let us look at what this might mean for Easter. Easter has commonly been regarded by Christians as the miraculous return of a dead man to life—a notion that Bishop David Jenkins called a travesty that turns Easter into a piece of cheap science fiction. Easter is very much greater than that.

Thirty-five years ago I wrote *Resurrection- A Symbol of Hope*, a book that traces the long development of the Easter message. The theme is not uniquely Christian, but permeated the religion of the ancient Middle East long before the rise of Christianity. Christians did not create the Easter message, but used it to interpret the tragic death of Jesus in positive terms of hope.

OUT OF DEATH COMES LIFE

The essential message of Easter can be put in the form of a paradox: All life ends in death, but out of death there also comes new life. The theme of death followed by resurrection had long found expression in the stories of the gods—stories we today call myths—and chief among them was the story of the dying-and-rising god.

The ancients told these stories because that is how they experienced life. They saw the sun die every day in the West and rise again with new life the next morning. They saw the moon wax and wane every month. Then for a short time it could not be seen at all. But on the third day the new moon appeared. That, by the way, is the origin of the well-known biblical phrase, "on the third day."

Then they noted the seasons of the year. The summer fruiting was followed by the autumn harvesting and then by the dying of vegetation in the winter. But in spring, what seemed to be dead came to life again. That is why the Easter festival was celebrated in spring. In spring, more strikingly than at any other time, death was being followed by resurrection to new life.

And not only in vegetation! Human life also ends in death. We too flourish like the grass, then wither and die, as the Psalmist observed. But as each generation passes away, it is succeeded by a new generation. Death and resurrection are built into the very fabric of all life on earth, including human life. This is the way Easter was celebrated for many centuries by the peoples of the ancient Middle East. The ancient Israelites reflected it in their own writings.

In Hosea, for example, we read:

Come, let us return to the Lord,
for he has torn us but he will heal us;
he has struck us but he will bind up our wounds.
After two days he will revive us;
on the third day he will restore us to life,
that we may come alive in his presence.

THE RESURRECTION OF ISRAEL

But the Israelites seized upon the theme to interpret their own history. When they faced near extinction as a people by being overrun by powerful empires, they drew on the ancient hope of resurrection. That is why we find the prophet Ezekiel expressing hope for

Israel's resurrection in the well-known vision of the valley of dry bones. "These bones are the whole house of Israel! Behold, says the Lord God, I will open your graves and raise you from your graves. I will put my spirit within you and you shall live and I will place you in your own land."

The prophet applied the renewal observable in the natural world to the ongoing destiny of his people. And once enunciated, that application of the "Easter" experience came to the fore every time the people of Israel faced new threats. In the middle of the second century BCE, Greek rulers tried to destroy the Jewish people and stamp out their traditions. That's when the Book of Daniel was written, a text in which we read this obviously inspiring promise: "There shall be a time of great trouble, but your people shall be delivered and those who sleep in the dust of the earth shall awake and the wise among them shall shine like the stars for ever."

Thus Easter faith—resurrection from the dead—was much talked about in Jewish circles at the beginning of the Christian era. It was an inherent part of the context of Jesus' ministry, and he debated it with his fellow Jews. Therefore, when he himself died on the cross as a martyr, his followers already had to hand the appropriate language with which to express their conviction that what Jesus represented to them could never be vanquished. Jesus was not dead, he was alive! But he was alive in a new way. He was alive in them. It was Paul our earliest written witness to the resurrection of Jesus who eloquently exclaimed, "It is no longer I who live but Christ who lives in me." And that explains why he came to speak of the community of Christians who shared this experience as the very "body of Christ." The historical Jesus had died, but all that he stood for was very much alive. The Church itself was the embodied risen Christ.

NOTHING NEW UNDER THE SUN

You may think that the Easter experiences of the first Christians was of an order quite different from the nature festivals of the past. The first Christians did not think so. Indeed, the Fourth Gospel places these words in the mouth of Jesus: "Truly, truly, I say to you, unless a grain of wheat falls into the earth and dies, it remains alone; but if it dies, it bears much fruit." In other words, the death of Jesus had been understood as analogous to the death of a seed that springs into new life.

Listen to how Clement, one of the very early Popes of Rome, put it: "Let us observe how the Creator is continually displaying the resurrection, of which we find an example in his raising of the Lord Jesus Christ from the dead. Let us look at the resurrection that happens regularly all the time. Day and night shows a resurrection; the night goes to sleep, the day rises: the day departs, night comes on. Let us take the crops. How does the sowing happen and in what way? The seed falls on the ground and dies. Then from the death of the one grain, by the mightiness of divine providence, there grows much more fruit."

If even the early Christians could see that the rising of Jesus from the dead was all of a piece with the death and resurrection to be observed within nature, how much more are we free to do so today. Now we can not only observe that life on this planet has an awe-inspiring capacity to keep renewing itself, but that the evolution of life in all of its innumerable and diverse forms out of this once life-less planet is itself the greatest resurrection miracle of all.

Even that is not the end of it. As astronomers now begin to unfold to us the marvels and mystery of our ever-evolving cosmos, they tell us that the earliest galaxies and stars did not yet have within them the chemical elements of carbon and the like that are essential to life. Before these more complex elements could even be created, stars of the type known as a supernovas had to explode and die, for only out of their fragments could the planets and the higher chemical elements be born. That is death and resurrection on the grand scale.

ONE GRAND MOTIF

Thus the universe itself is deeply permeated by this basic phenomenon of death and resurrection. The Easter theme of life

out of non-life—of life, death and resurrection—has been opera-
tive from the beginning of time. It is inherent in the nature of
the universe itself and a fundamental principle of all life on this
planet. This wellspring of existence as we know it surely calls for
continual celebration.

What an opportunity this ecological age offers for green
Christianity to restore to Easter celebrations the eternal message
of Easter! It is something to give us hope as we face an imminent
ecological crisis. Just as our own bodies show a remarkable capacity
to recover after illness and disease, so the earth has a remarkable
capacity to recover, to regain its stability, to renew itself. We can
take heart from the fact that the creative forces within us, within
nature, and within the universe itself, are of such a kind that a
new earth can yet be resurrected out of the death with which we
humans currently threaten it. Easter, thus celebrated, can revive in
us the hope for a worthwhile future on this planet.

Now let us turn to Christmas. For some 1500 years the 25ᵗʰ of
December has been celebrated as the birthday of Jesus Christ, but
that was not the case early on. It is now widely accepted that we
know neither the day nor the year in which Jesus was born. But
in about the fifth century Christians took over and Christianized
an already existing nature festival—the one that marked the
winter solstice in the northern hemisphere. It celebrated the day
when the sun began to rise higher in the sky, bringing longer and
warmer days. This festival began as another version of the Easter
theme, and its slogan was *Sol Invictus*—The Unconquerable Sun.
Christians thought the words particularly apt for the celebration of
the new hope they associated with the coming of Jesus Christ.

The Christmas festival remains much more popular today than
Easter because, without any guidance from anyone, society has long
been unconsciously engaged in changing its character. Those who
wish to celebrate it as the birthday of the supposed Savior of the
world are still free to do so. But for the majority it no longer means
that. Even though the outward trappings remain—angelic choirs,
the shepherds, the Bethlehem manger, the Three Wise Men—
Christmas has become a time of giving and receiving gifts along

with outpourings of peace and goodwill. Above all, it is the one season of the year when families try to get together. This fostering of family life is to be encouraged and extended. It is a celebration of something very important in nature. Our very humanity, including the evolution of human culture, has been made possible by generation after generation of people being nurtured in families.

We in the southern hemisphere have special problems with both of these annual festivals. We celebrate Easter in the autumn, although it is in essence a spring festival. And Christmas is more appropriate in the winter, when the cold and darkness of the season encourage the family to move closer together around a burning fire in the hearth. Thus some pioneering souls in our hemisphere are already making attempts to mark the 21st of June with a winter solstice celebration. Such a move is to be encouraged in this ecological age. Should New Zealand become a republic, we could well replace Queen's Birthday weekend with the celebration of the winter solstice on the third Monday of June. This could be joined with the Maori New Year, Matariki, which was celebrated on the first new moon after the appearance on the north-eastern horizon of the cluster of stars called the Pleiades by the Greeks and Matariki by the Maori.

THE DAY OF RE-CREATION

Until modern times the Christian church has been the official promoter and guardian of our festivals. Unfortunately, however, because it became increasingly divorced from the natural world and interpreted human life in otherworldly terms, it now has a great deal of unlearning to do before it can give to our ecological age the spiritual guidance that is so badly needed. Paradoxically, the church must learn to discover and experience within itself its own most basic message. Like the Lord it proclaims, the church must be prepared to die to its former life in order that it may be resurrected to the new vitality demanded by the ecological age.

Before it is too late, the church must take the opportunity to reorient its own most frequent festival—the Sunday service. We have already noted that the seven-day week goes back to the ancient Canaanites, representing the basic unit of the Canaanite agricultural calendar. The chief reason for its survival through later Jewish, Christian, and Muslim tradition was the observation of one day in seven as a day of rest. It has been celebrated in a wide variety of ways through history—the Jewish Sabbath, the Christian Lord's Day, Muslim holy day, and now a secular holiday—but it has never lost its original beneficial purpose of providing a day of rest from normal work. That is why it was called the Sabbath, which means "cessation." Originally it entailed rest from labor not only for humans but for animals, and not only for creatures but for the land. The processes of nature also had to have their rest, if they were to continue produce their fruits for humankind. The existence of the sabbatical year shows that ancient Canaanite agriculturists had learned the value of letting land lie fallow.

In many respects the seven-day week, with the institution of one of them as a day of rest, is the most enduring cultural gift we have inherited from ancient Canaan. In spite of the overwhelming secularization of the Sabbath, this day of rest from work remains firmly embedded in our culture and, through Christian and Muslim influence, is now becoming a worldwide observance. What we are in danger of losing, however, is the positive spiritual direction it has in Judaism, Christianity, and Islam. Perhaps today we value rest from labor, whether mental or manual, more than ever; it provides for the re-creation of energy in mind and body. What Jew, Christian, and Muslim added to this by their various forms of worship was re-creation of spirit.

In order to get the most out of life, we need regular occasions for taking stock of ourselves, clarifying our aims, admitting our mistakes, and resolving to make a new beginning. This is what their various spiritual practices did for Jew, Christian, and Muslim in the past.

A NEW ORDER OF WORSHIP

If we are to respond constructively to the coming ecological crisis, re-orienting the Sunday service to the cause of green consciousness can play an important role. Less change would be needed than at first appears necessary. The service will still be a form of worship—that is, acknowledging what is of supreme worth to us. As Thomas Berry points out, "There is an awe and reverence due to the stars in the heavens, the sun and the heavenly bodies; to the seas and the continents; to all living forms of trees and flowers; to the myriad expressions of life in the sea; to the animals of the forest and the birds of the air. To wantonly destroy a living species is to silence forever a divine voice."

Reflecting on our cultural origins will still have its place; that is what Bible readings provided. Time will still be set aside for meditation; that is what the prayers provided. Mental stimulation, which is what the sermon provided, will remain an essential ingredient. It is the content rather than the form that needs to change. Ecological spirituality will focus on the nature of our relatedness, not only to one another as humans in human society, but also to all living forms of life in the ecosphere and to the forces of nature.

The singing of songs will still have an important place. You may think that what we sing is of no real significance. Not so! This may be illustrated by observing the rapid spread of the Protestant Reformation through northern Europe, for a great upsurge in congregational singing communicated the new spirit far more powerfully than could pulpit oratory or doctrinal tracts. Pope Urban III complained that Martin Luther had sung the church into heresy. In a similar way the evangelical revival under the Wesley brothers was spread by hymn lyrics. To this day the religious beliefs of churchgoers are shaped more by the hymns they sing than by the sermons they hear. It has been well said that religion is not so much taught as caught. And already appropriate hymns are being composed—many of them by New Zealand's best-known hymn writer, Shirley Murray.

The reformed Sunday worship will also celebrate everything we have come to value in human existence, such as the importance of healthy human relationships and the rich inheritance of human culture. In these days of declining church attendance, the reason why some still go to church despite the obsolete nature of the words often used, is the fellowship and mutual support they find there.

CHANGE IN THE PRACTICES

We should note in this respect the great change that has already taken place in the way Christians celebrate their central ritual, known variously as Holy Communion, the Lord's Supper, the Mass, or the Eucharist. Over the last four centuries it has been interpreted less and less as the commemoration of a sacrifice offered on an altar to God (as it was in the Middle Ages) and more and more as the sharing of a common meal. Even the Catholic Church has made significant moves in this direction since the Vatican II Council. This ritual originated among the ancient Semitic nomads, who placed great emphasis on hospitality. It has gone through many forms, for better or for worse, but it can still celebrate and nurture the rich and sacred character of human fellowship.

The ritual that has changed most during the twentieth century has been the funeral service. It is fast ceasing to be the official "send-off" to the next world and is becoming the celebration of a life lived in this world. Similarly, though the alteration has barely begun, the ritual of infant baptism can be profitably changed: once seen as the business of cleansing from original sin, it can easily become the welcome of new life into the family. And confirmation will become a ritual by which adolescents acknowledge their adult responsibilities both to their fellow-humans and to the ecosphere.

As the religious activities of the past are reformed to meet the needs of the ecological age, more and more forms, equivalent to those of the past but relevant to life in the present, will be created and widely adopted. One of the great creations of the past is what we know as the Ten Commandments. This formula has lasted so long largely because it was once such an inspired creation, and indeed there are frequent calls to return to it. But however appropriate it may have been in the past, its relevance in the ecological age is much diminished, not least because even the word "Commandment" is no longer suitable. Today we are free people who choose our behavior out of inner conviction. Nevertheless, as Green Christianity responds to the ecological imperative, it may well compose statements of intent to replace the creeds of the past.

NOW, THEREFORE, BE IT RESOLVED . . .

Let me conclude, then, by offering *Ten Resolutions* which could help us build a healthy world to hand on to those who follow us.

1. Let us take time to stand in awe of this self-evolving universe.
2. Let us marvel at the living ecosphere of this planet.
3. Let us set a supreme value on all forms of life.
4. Let us develop a lifestyle that preserves the balance of the planetary eco-system.
5. Let us refrain from all activities that endanger the future of any species.
6. Let us devote ourselves to maximizing the future for all living creatures.
7. Let us set the needs of the coming global society before those of ourselves, our tribe, society, or nation.
8. Let us learn to value the human relationships that bind us together into social groups.
9. Let us learn to appreciate the total cultural legacy we have received from the past.
10. Let us accept in a self-sacrificing fashion the responsibility now laid upon us all for the future of our species and of all planetary life.

So ends this sketch of the greening of Christianity.

IN PRAISE OF THE SECULAR

10

WHAT DOES "SECULAR" MEAN?

The title of this series, "In Praise of the Secular," was suggested to me by that of a book written as long ago as 1509. It was called *In Praise of Folly* and was written by Erasmus (1466–1536), the most famous scholar of the Renaissance. Although of Dutch origin, he lived and worked in many places in Europe. In fact, when he wrote that little book he was staying in London with Sir Thomas More, and the Latin title was an intended pun on his host's name. (*Moriae Encomium* could be taken to mean "in praise of folly" or "in praise of More.") Although he wrote this 150–page work in a week, it had been forming in his mind while he was travelling on horseback from Italy to England.

A MAN OF MANY HUMORS . . .

The book is a witty satire in the form of a long address by a personified Folly. By this means Erasmus engaged in a merciless critique of church practices, monastic activities, and scholastic theology. For example, he says of the monks (of whom he had himself been one), "they bray like donkeys in church, repeating by rote the psalms they have not understood, imagining they are charming the ears of their heavenly audience with infinite delight."

Because it was intended as a bit of light-hearted tomfoolery (not even Erasmus ever regarded it highly), the book enabled him to say things about church life that he could not even have hinted at in a serious dissertation. But his words had the same effect as those of the little boy of the fairy tale who exclaimed, "The Emperor has no clothes on." In the end, ironically, this little satire became his most famous work.

Rather than a philosopher or theologian, Erasmus was chiefly a biblical scholar and a linguist; yet he is widely regarded as the spiritual ancestor of much modern religious thought. He poked fun at the scholastic theology of the day for being quite out of touch with daily life, for he was more concerned with the Sermon on the Mount and ethical religion than with theological niceties. More than most, he was acutely aware of the need for radical reform in the church.

Indeed, it was often said, "Erasmus laid the egg that Luther hatched." Yet, when Martin Luther's challenging acts led to the sudden outbreak of reforming activities, Erasmus held himself aloof from them. This was partly because he was a mild and somewhat timid man. As the illegitimate son of a priest, he had not known the joy and consolation of the family experience, and throughout his life craved affection and appreciation. My teacher John Dickie passed on to us the venerable quip that Erasmus appeared to have descended from a long line of maiden aunts—though today some might find that witticism "politically insensitive."

At first Erasmus found much to affirm in what Luther was saying, but he became offended by Luther's "extremism and rough manners." Moreover, he had no wish to offend the new Pope, Adrian VI, who was also a Dutchman and an old school friend of Erasmus. Adrian was a reforming Pope who tried to stop the sale of the indulgences that had sparked off the Protestant Reformation. Unfortunately, he died prematurely after only a year in office, worn out by the many and difficult problems he faced. Had he lived, church history might have been very different.

That very year Erasmus wrote a diatribe against Luther, entitling it *On Freewill*. He dismissed the excessive confidence in human moral strength held by the Pelagians, but he equally rejected the theory—expounded by Augustine and defended by Luther—of the essential hopelessness of the human condition. Luther was furious with Erasmus, and wrote a reply four times as long, condemning the open-minded middle way proposed by Erasmus. "We *must* go to extremes," concluded Luther; "we *must* deny free will altogether and ascribe everything to God." Erasmus, unable to persuade his critics to adopt a mediating position between these extremist positions, and finding himself condemned by Protestant and Catholic alike, retired from the public controversy.

By now you will no doubt suspect that I have borrowed from Erasmus more that a couple of words for the title of this series; I have briefly described his role in an ancient controversy in order to throw some light on what is the chief area of religious debate today. We are no longer involved in a bitter conflict between Catholic and Protestant, for a great deal of mutual respect and understanding now exists between these two elements of Western religious culture—a respect that was entirely absent in the sixteenth and seventeenth centuries.

THE MORE THINGS CHANGE . . .

Indeed, the chief religious conflicts today are not among the major world religions. Rather, it is between those who call themselves religious and those who regard themselves as secular. This great divide, I suggest, is today's equivalent of the Protestant-Catholic conflict at the time of the Reformation. In those days Catholics and Protestants each claimed to possess the ultimate truth, and fiercely condemned their opponents as the servants of Satan. Today it is the followers of traditional religions and the militant secularists who pour scorn on one another, treating their opponents as dangerous enthusiasts who must be silenced at all costs for the future good of humanity.

Fundamentalists, whether Christian or Muslim, regard all things secular as the work of Satan, as undermining what they regard as the ultimate and eternal truths revealed by God. Militant secularists, on the other hand, regard all traditional religious beliefs and practices as the results of grotesque superstitions that should be eradicated as harmful anachronisms. Recently, examples of this extremist secularism have been coming off the press in quick succession: *The God Delusion* by Richard Dawkins, *God is not Great* by Christopher Hitchens, and *The End of Faith* by Sam Harris.

Like Erasmus of old I want to explore the issues and develop a mediating position in this conflict. Just as he held up to ridicule the traditional beliefs and practices of the church of his day, so I concede that there is much in traditional Christianity that deserves Dawkins' trenchant criticism. A number of the stories, injunctions, and doctrines we find in the Bible are so morally repugnant that we should not hesitate to declare them so.

Furthermore much of the dogma still affirmed by the church and practiced in its rituals is better termed superstition than genuine religion. I define superstition as any belief or practice that has out-lived the cultural context in which it was once appropriate. These dogmas and rituals are outmoded and superstitious because they were shaped to reflect a view of the world that began to disappear from our common knowledge and experience three or four centuries ago.

By their blanket rejection of everything in the religions of the past, however, militant secularists throw out the baby with the bathwater in their disregard for the beneficial spiritual and moral values also nurtured by these traditions. Although Dawkins is one who errs considerably in this respect, he nevertheless attempts to rescue himself. Right at the end of his book he declares that he is "a little taken aback at the biblical ignorance displayed by people in more recent decades" and makes a final plea that we do not lose touch with the "treasured heritage" of our cultural past.

I intend to expound a mediating position between the funda-mentalists and the militant secularists by showing that they both have a faulty understanding of the secular. Fundamentalists see the secular as an enemy to their faith and way of life, but I wish to say something in praise of the secular. Militant secularists, for their part, have also misunderstood what secularism really is, and have declared war on anything associated with religion. As a result, the word "secular" is commonly taken to mean "anti-religious," some-thing it did not originally signify at all.

. . . THE MORE THEY NEED EXPLAINING

Let us go back, then, to the etymology of "secular." Derived from the Latin *saeculum*, which means "an age" or "a lifetime," the word came to mean "this age or world in which we live." During the centuries when Latin was the *lingua franca* of medieval academic Christendom, *saeculum* was used to translate the Hebrew '*olam* and Greek *aeon*, words found in such biblical phrases as "from one age to another" or "for ever and ever." In medieval Latin this phrase became *ad saecula saeculorum*, and Christians were well accustomed to hearing it in the liturgy of the mass. It is further interesting to note that those in monasteries and convents were known as "the religious"—since they lived by a strict communal rule—whereas parish priests were known as "the seculars"—for they lived and worked in the world, as did all their faithful parishioners.

To recapture the original meaning of "secular," then, one might propose that its nearest synonym is "this-worldly" and its antonym is "otherworldly." For clearly the modern world has brought a steady increase in our knowledge and understanding of "this-world"—that is, the physical, tangible world. In particular, the discoveries of Galileo, Newton, and Einstein have caused the "other-world" of the heavens to become merged with the "this-world" of our space-time universe. All this has led to a steady decrease in our interest in, or convictions about, any unseen and therefore hypothetical "other-world." It has even given rise to such quips as "He is so otherworldly that he's no longer of any earthly use."

This process of switching attention from the "other-world" to "this-world" is what is meant by the word "secularization." It was about 1864 when the word first came into usage to describe the process of cultural change that was by then becoming clearly discernible. One hundred years later the theologian Harvey Cox wrote his widely read book *The Secular City*, in which he described "secularization" quite succinctly as "man turning his attention away from worlds beyond and toward this world and this time."

But it must be obvious that turning one's attention away from supposed other worlds to this world and this time does not necessarily mean one is no longer concerned with religion. Indeed the Israelite prophets were very much concerned with this world. In no uncertain terms they called for justice in the market place and peace among the nations. Hence the process of secularization should not be regarded as an anti-religious movement. Actually, it leaves the future of religion an open question.

WANTED: SECULAR SAINTS

This point was made in a lecture as long ago as 1850 by W. B. Hodgson on "The Secular, the Religious and the Theological," in which he said, "Secular means belonging to the Saeculum or Age, or *period* of life on this earth, as distinguished from eternity or life to come. It should never have come to mean the opposite of *religious*. The fact that something may be described as secular does not preclude it from also being religious."

To make this clearer, however, we must turn our attention briefly to what constitutes religion. Because we are in the midst of a period of rapid and far-reaching cultural change, most people think of religion in terms that are far too narrow, identifying it with something they have known from the past. And theologians themselves have sometimes been guilty of that same error. For example, the great twentieth century theologian Karl Barth, in attempting to expound a contemporary Christian faith, declared that Christianity is not a religion. And following his mentor, the even more radical Dietrich Bonhoeffer coined the phrase "religionless Christianity"—a term that was later and more appropriately translated as "secular Christianity."

Even most of the definitions of religion listed in the Oxford Dictionary have become far too narrow. It says, for example, "Religion is the human recognition of superhuman controlling power and especially of a personal God entitled to obedience." Only the fifth and last definition it offers is at all satisfactory: "Religion is action that one feels bound to do." That definition comes from the etymology of the word, for the root from which comes the Latin *religio* means " to bind."

Acknowledging the confusion that surrounds the word "religion" today, W. Cantwell Smith wrote a seminal little book in 1962, *The Meaning and End of Religion*. There he showed that the popular use of the term to refer to a specific set of beliefs and practices, particularly with a supernatural dimension, is quite modern. Indeed, its derivation shows that it did not originally refer to any particular set of beliefs at all, but to the degree of commitment or devotion that people displayed towards their most important interests. For that reason, the word was never used in the plural as we do today when we talk about "the religions of the world."

PURE RELIGION AND UNDEFILED

Religio, and hence "religion," basically meant conscientiousness—and, more specifically, "a conscientious concern for what really matters." This is what Paul Tillich was recovering for the word when he defined religion as "the state of being grasped by an ultimate concern, a concern which qualifies all other concerns as preliminary and which itself contains the answer to the question of the meaning of life." Carlo Della Casa, an Italian scholar of modern religion, put it even more simply: "Religion is a total mode of the interpreting and living of life."

Smith suggested that in the current confusion we should stop talking about "religion" and "religions," and instead fasten our attention on the capacity of people to be religious. In this sense an atheist like Richard Dawkins, who is sincerely and passionately protesting against the traditional understanding of God out of a concern for truth, is to be judged more religious than those nominal Christians who have at best a half-hearted commitment to the God they claim to believe in.

Further, Smith asserted that we should stop thinking of religion as a "thing"—something consisting of beliefs, rituals, holy scriptures, moral codes and so on—that we may choose to embrace or reject. He called such a complex of individual and shared elements the "cumulative tradition" of a particular path trodden by people on the religious quest. As but one of many routes, it is not to be confused with the religious quest itself, for it is simply the collective behavior of people who walk a particular pathway of faith. Being a product of the inherent religious dimension of human existence, it must always remain secondary to the continuing religious quest itself.

Humans show themselves to be religious whenever and wherever they take the questions of human existence seriously, and then create a common response to whatever they find to be of ultimate value to them. The only truly non-religious person is one who treats human existence as trivial or meaningless, for ultimately the religious phenomenon arises out of human experience as we reflect on the fundamental nature of human existence. With but rare exceptions, people everywhere and at all times have made some kind of response to the demands of human existence. They have tried to make something of life. They have looked for meaning and purpose. They have hoped for some kind of fulfillment. For such reasons humankind has in the past been universally religious, and there is no good reason to suspect that in the future people will cease to be religious. And this is true even though an increasing number have grown dissatisfied with the religious forms of the past, having found them to be irrelevant in the new cultural age we have entered.

WHERE DO *YOU* LIVE?

Therefore let us now look at the cultural features that mark our times as a new age. I shall attempt to explain this in terms of our worldview—the way we see, or understand, the world in which we live. Do we all live in the same world? Yes and no! Common sense keeps telling us that we do. But what we see or understand as "the world out there" turns out to be a mental image within our heads; it is a world we have unconsciously interpreted. That interpreted "reality" is our worldview. Indeed, we are always one step removed from the objective universe. "Our world," the world to which we respond in the way we live, is not simple reality itself (whatever that might be) but reality understood and interpreted through the grid of our language and culture. The only world we "know" with our minds and talk about with one another is a world we have already interpreted.

Thus each of us has his or her own worldview, and being personal and unique to each, it differs slightly from person to person. It exists in our minds as a complex set of mental images that we accumulate during life. Two main sources furnish the material from which we construct our worldviews. The first is personal experience gained through our senses—chiefly sight, touch and sound. The second is the interpretations with which we clothe the data that we receive through our senses. Through language, for example, we name what we see. This immediately gives us a psy-chological sense of security and even of power, for we feel we know something when we name it and thus accept it into our world. What we cannot name we tend to regard as mysterious, foreign, and potentially dangerous.

But we do more than name the objects we encounter. We connect them together into a unified world in which we discern some meaning or purpose. To do this, we are mainly dependent upon the culture into which we are born. Each culture is distinguished not only by its language, but by a general worldview that it shares and passes on from generation to generation.

This explains why we live in a new cultural age, one that is increasingly global and secular: our various common worldviews have been undergoing radical changes. Let me sketch the new worldview that came to birth in Western Europe and then began to spread all over the globe—and that explains why today people everywhere see the world rather differently than did their ancestors in the sixteenth century.

CONSTRUCTING A
NEW WORLD

These, then, are the main phases through which this new worldview began to take shape after 1600. First, one can hardly overemphasize the contributions of Copernicus and Galileo. They were the pioneers of the space age. They displaced our human home— planet earth—from the center of the universe around which everything revolved and made it a tiny and almost insignificant speck in a physical universe too vast for us to contain in our mind's eye. All educated people around the world are now aware of the space-time universe in which we humans live.

Second, Galileo's telescope made it clear that the moon was of much the same material as the earth. Such a discovery was soon to lead to the conviction that the sun, the stars and the nebulae are all of a piece with this earth. From Newton onwards we came to understand that this almost infinite physical universe everywhere operates by the same basic laws of nature. That meant that what was once long regarded as the **super**natural area of space had now been brought within the sphere of the natural. "This-world" had suddenly expanded to swallow up what had been traditionally conceived as "other-world." That was secularization with a vengeance!

The heavens, or sky above, had long been seen as God's own domain. "Our Father who art in heaven," begins the Lord's prayer. It had also come to be seen as the dwelling place of the blessed departed Galileo's discoveries meant that God had become deprived of his holy dwelling space, and the souls of the dead had no actual *place* to go to. Most of us have so unquestioningly accepted this that we regarded as quite silly the observation of the first Russian astronaut that he found no evidence of God in outer space. And as even Pope John Paul II was forced to concede, "Heaven is not a *place*; it is a state of mind." No wonder that even in Galileo's time the church sensed that his claims had such far-reaching consequences that it seemed appropriate to silence him.

What gradually took place in the collective European mind over the next few centuries was telescoped into one day for a Papuan whom I once heard tell his personal story. He said his tribe had always believed that their dead continued to live on after death in the next valley, a place separated from them by an immense mountain range. Then came the time when white strangers arrived and took him on a journey through this mysterious valley, and he was stunned and shocked to find it similar to his homeland and the dead ancestors nowhere to be seen. What happened in a single day for that Papuan, had slowly seeped into the collective European mind over three centuries as it came to understand the significance of Galileo's discoveries.

And while we have had nearly four hundred years to change our worldview in the light of Galileo and the later cosmologists, we have had much less time to adjust to the second great shift in our worldview. This important milestone was largely the work of Charles Darwin. As Galileo made the universe all of a piece with the earth, Darwin taught us to see the human species as related to all other earthly creatures. As the earth was no longer the center of the universe, so the human species was no longer the special creation—half-animal half divine—that our forbears had long supposed it to be. We humans now know ourselves to be but one of the millions of species that have emerged on this planet. We are all part of the complex, still mysterious, evolving world of nature.

CAST ADRIFT IN
THE COSMOS

Galileo and Darwin are only the two foremost representatives of the rising tide of scientists who have been collectively responsible for the radical changes that have taken place in our worldviews. Empirical science began to enunciate a series of natural laws that explain how the world of nature operates without recourse to any external force. The more they did this, the less room was left for God to perform his miracles. For a while scientists looked for gaps in the system. Even Newton did. But as "this-world" became more and more self-explanatory, the effect was to ease out of the picture altogether the God who had long been understood as the all-powerful, personal creator. And all this has been part of the process of secularization.

As empirical knowledge rapidly grew and spread—particularly between the middle of the nineteenth century and the middle of the twentieth century—it became common to think of religion and science as bitter enemies of one another. This apparent conflict was partly due to the popular misunderstanding of both science and religion. Let me now attempt to sort this issue out.

When we speak of science today, we are referring to empiricism, by which we mean knowledge that has survived a variety of tests without being disproved. The application of such tests is a method that has gradually improved and widened in its scope, but this should not hide from us the fact that the word "science" still basically means knowledge.

The classical age of empirical science was preceded by a long period of what we may call cultural knowledge. Each culture accumulated in the course of its history a body of knowledge that it passed on from generation to generation—information that had survived the test of general experience. But confidence in the validity of that knowledge often rested on appeal to the authority of the past. And the culturally transmitted "body of knowledge" included everything from the origin of the world to the medical cure of diseases. It is anachronistic to refer to its elements as either religion or science, for such a modern distinction could not be made before the emergence of empirical science.

HAS GOD LOST HIS JOB?

Let me illustrate this by reference to the opening chapter of Genesis. Here we are told that in the space of six days God created everything that exists, from light to human beings. This is no more religious knowledge than it is scientific knowledge. It originated as a cultural theory in a Jewish context and was a great advance on the earlier Jewish story of origins—the one preserved in chapters 2 and 3 of that same book.

To appreciate the significance of the Genesis 1 hypothesis, we need to look at it in the light of modern science. Physicists today have discerned four basic forces—gravitational force, electromagnetic force, the weak nuclear force, and the strong nuclear force. They are now looking for what they call the Grand Unified Theory, which they hope will link them all together. If successful they would then have uncovered what is referred to as a Theory of Everything. Now that is exactly what Genesis 1 is—an attempt to explain why everything is the way it is by referring it all to one basic force called God. This theory explained the origin of light, of day and night, the seasons of the year, and the creation of all living things.

This theory was first enunciated in ancient Babylon about 450 BCE, and eventually replaced all earlier and more primitive explanations. The unknown author of it could be described as a Jewish "scientist," as brilliant in his day as the much later Einstein was in his. It was so brilliant that for the next two and a half thousand years it convinced nearly everybody who heard it. It still convinces many today, partly because it is so simple, neat and tidy. Christian fundamentalists still defend it by such explanations and subsidiary expositions as "Creation Science" and "Intelligent Design." What they are defending is neither religious knowledge nor scientific knowledge, but ancient cultural knowledge which, brilliant though it was at the time, no longer stands up to the tests being used by today's empirical scientists.

A NEW DISPENSATION

The worldview that has been arising as a result of Galileo, Darwin, and science generally is now spreading round the globe. This is because the intellectual disciplines of physics, chemistry, geology, biology, and cosmology are the same the world over. They transcend nationality and the knowledge previously transmitted in traditional cultures. The basic human knowledge that constitutes the raw material of our worldview is fast becoming the same for everybody. It has become secular and global.

Secular knowledge is knowledge of the physical, tangible world gained and tested by empirical science. The more this way of learning has enabled us to understand the world in which we live by enunciating the basic laws by which it operates, the less room can be found for anything that could be called *super*natural. Indeed, for increasing numbers of people the very idea of the supernatural has been completely eased out of their view of the world.

In later lectures I shall be drawing attention first to the many personal and social benefits we all accept and enjoy within the new secular world, and after that to its consequences for religion and spirituality. But in the next lecture I shall discuss how it was out of Christendom that the secular world emerged. Today's world has resulted from the pioneering efforts of creative Christian thinkers.

11

THE EMERGENCE OF
THE SECULAR AGE

E arly in the twentieth century the celebrated poet T. S. Eliot wrote these words in his "Choruses from the Rock":

> But it seems that something has happened that has never happened before: though we know not just when, or why, or how, or where. Men have left God not for other gods, they say, but for no god; and this has never happened before.

This "something" did not happen all of a sudden. It was a cultural transformation that had been on its way for a very long time, and only quite recently had its approach accelerated and its imminent arrival become evident. The *Encyclopaedia Britannica* referred to this phenomenon as secularization and described it thus: "a movement in society directed away from other-worldliness to this-worldliness. In the medieval period there was a strong tendency for religious persons to despise human affairs and to meditate on God and the afterlife. As a reaction to this medieval tendency, secularization, at the time of the Renaissance, exhibited itself in the development of humanism, when humans began to show more interest in human cultural development and the possibilities of fulfillment in this world. The movement towards secularization has been in progress during the entire course of modern history."

A REALLY OLD-TIME RELIGION

I suggest that with the gift of hindsight we can now trace the process of secularization as far back as the First Axial Period, 800–200 BCE—the era to which all the great religious traditions of the modern world can trace their roots. Of course it appears not only paradoxical but even absurd to suggest that the great world religions had in them the seeds of the secularization that would eventually bring about their dissolution. So how could this be?

In the cultural era that preceded the First Axial Period—at least 100,000 years in length—our ancient human ancestors were not aware of embracing any religion at all. What they lived by was a labyrinth of myths and rituals that each tribe or ethnic group had slowly accumulated. This body of knowledge taught them they were living in a world owned and controlled by unseen spirits and gods. These could be both beneficent and hostile, and were very unpredictable. Humans did not yet see themselves inhabiting a world they could call their own.

The myths and rituals by which pre-Axial peoples understood and responded to the world were believed to have descended unchanged from the mythical time of origins—the beginning-time. They embodied the unchangeable truth of the world, and this had to be observed and passed on unaltered. Pre-Axial cultures were thus typified by an intrinsic conservatism that both legitimated and preserved the *status quo*. Any innate urge of the human spirit for creative enquiry was severely repressed by a cultural system that was committed to the avoidance of all change.

That is why the Axial Period was such an unexpected phenomenon. Karen Armstrong entitled her recent book about it *The Great Transformation*, for this was a time when a few daring souls such as Zarathustra, the Buddha, Confucius, the Israelite prophets, and the Greek philosophers began to question the cultural knowledge they had inherited. So creative and productive were their reflections that they were instrumental in (at least) a partial emancipation of humankind from the prison of static cultures. And in doing so they gave birth to traditions that possessed important new characteristics.

A BRAVE NEW WORLD

First, instead of focusing exclusively on the gods, as had been done hitherto, the new traditions began to honor human figures. I refer to such people as Moses, the Buddha, Confucius, Plato, Jesus, and Muhammad. These historical figures were now allotted prominent and exalted places, as is evident from the myths central to the new cultures. Whereas the myths of the pre-Axial cultures had been set in a supra-mundane world and the chief figures were the gods, those of the First Axial Period and thereafter were clearly grounded in **this** world and focused on historical human figures.

In Judaism Moses led the people of Israel to freedom and received the divine Law on Mt. Sinai. In Buddhism Gautama experienced enlightenment under the Bo tree. In Christianity Jesus' crucifixion became the source of divine grace. In Islam Muhammad received the Qur'an from the angel Gabriel. The basic myths of the post-Axial traditions focused on events and people in human history rather than supernatural events in another world. And by setting in *this* world the myths by which people live meaningful lives, they were taking the first steps in the process of secularization.

Second, the awareness of personal freedom and responsibility so characteristic of the modern secular world also arose at this time. Until then one had no religious choice, for one's basic beliefs were intrinsic elements of the culture one was born into. That changed in the Axial Period. To become a Buddhist, Christian, or Muslim, one had to make a deliberate choice; indeed, the act of making such a choice is part and parcel of ritual practice in those three traditions, as exemplified by baptism and confirmation in Christianity. Further, because these new traditions could be embraced, they could also be rejected. The need to make such a choice showed that a person's destiny was now, in part at least, in one's own hands and not wholly in the hands of the gods or other external forces as was the case hitherto.

Third, the new role being played by human choice now meant that the rest of a culture was open to change and development at a faster pace than ever before. Whereas the pre-Axial cultures abhorred change, the post-Axial religious traditions not only initiated it, but anticipated even more in the future. Christianity looked for the coming of the Kingdom of God and Islam for the global brotherhood of all people. Thus the new religious cultures not only had a beginning in time, but also exhibited lives and histories in a way that pre-Axial cultures did not.

After the initial cultural transformation from the old to the new had taken place, however, the ancient distrust of novelty began to re-assert itself, and the new revelations themselves came to be regarded as final and absolute. The Torah contained 613 laws that Jews must obey for all time; the Christian Bible came to be seen as a repository of eternal truth; and the Qur'an contained the revealed Word of God that no Muslim must ever question.

YOU CAN'T KEEP A GOOD MOVEMENT DOWN

Even so, the new cultural ferment, the questioning and creativity that had emerged during the Axial Period, could not be repressed forever. The resulting restlessness reappeared chiefly within the Christian tradition. It is a fact beyond dispute that the modern secular world emerged out of Western Christendom, but that does not explain why the secular world was born in the West and not, say, in the Islamic or the Buddhist world. To be sure, human history does not operate according to the simple laws of cause and effect that govern the physical world, for insignificant events often appear to trigger off major historical movements.

But having acknowledged that general principle, I now wish to point to some traits unique to the Judeo-Christian tradition— or at least more prominent there than elsewhere—that may help to explain why modern secularism emerged out of the Christian world. Indeed, I shall suggest that secularization is the logical consequence of specific elements in the Judeo-Christian tradition, and that this is true even though the majority of contemporary Christians do not see it that way and commonly treat secularization as an enemy to be feared and overcome.

Already in 1967, when I was writing *God in the New World*, I was contending that the seeds of the new secular culture are to be found in the Judeo-Christian tradition itself. I pointed out, for example, that what makes the Bible unique among the holy books of the great world religions is its concern with history. The Cambridge historian, Herbert Butterfield, had said of the Old Testament, "we have here the greatest and most deliberate attempts ever made to wrestle with destiny and interpret history and discover meaning in the human drama." In fact, the Old Testament's primary portrait of God is not as the Creator of the natural world, but rather as the Lord of history. In this way the Bible shifted attention away from the unseen realm of the gods to the historical this-worldly scene where we live out our lives.

THE OLD ORDER CHANGETH

The theologian Harvey Cox argued in his widely read book, *The Secular City*, that secularization is the legitimate consequence of the impact of the Old Testament on world history. The Hebrew doctrine of creation, he said, was the beginning of the disenchantment of the world of nature. The Hebrew insurrection in Egypt, leading to the Exodus under Moses, was the beginning of the desacralization of politics. The prohibition of graven images was the beginning of what he called the "deconsecration of values." Similarly the New Testament scholar Rudolf Bultmann claimed that "Christianity itself was a decisive factor in the development of the secularization of the world in that it de-divinized the world."

The sociologist Peter Berger likewise asserted that "the roots of secularization are to be found in the earliest available sources for the religion of Israel." It thus appears that while modern secularization came to birth in the Christian West, its roots seem to be in the ancient Jewish heritage out of which Christianity itself sprang. By retaining the Hebrew Bible as the major part of its scriptural canon—even though much of that heritage lay dormant until the Reformation—Christianity never became divorced from its Jewish origins.

Then Christians, influenced by the Jewish concern with history, were led to divide history into BC and AD (before and after Christ) and to envision the end of history and the coming of a new world. Since history was seen as the unfolding of a meaningful story about this world, it is not at all surprising that the Christian West gave rise to the much more extensive story of cosmic and biological evolution, bringing with it our modern acceptance of change and development as being inherent aspects of life and reality.

And while yet in its infancy, Christianity gave rise to an article of faith that can be interpreted as a continuation of the secularizing forces present within ancient Israel—the distinctive and central doctrine of the Incarnation. What early Christians wished to affirm by the Incarnation was their conviction that Jesus of Nazareth was a meeting point between humankind and God. Although fully human, Jesus spoke with all the authority of God. Moreover, he embodied in human form all the divine qualities—the grace and truth of God. The important implication of this tenet for our present purposes lies in its assertion that the human condition can be conceived as capable of embodying the divine nature and manifesting the divine attributes. When looked at in this way, the doctrine of the Incarnation may be regarded as a further step in secularization; for it states not only that the transcendent God is to be found *within* the physical world rather than *outside* of it, but that the divine has become manifest in the human condition.

MAKING HASTE SLOWLY

Such a thought eventually proved too daring even for most Christians, and as time went on Christianity developed an interpretation of the Incarnation that was almost the negation of its original intention. The reason for this lay in a theological conflict: it had become virtually impossible to root out the ancient view (the so-called "Gnostic heresy") that conceived Jesus to be an eternal, divine, and supernatural figure who had once walked the earth *in the form* of a man, but had never really been *completely* human and had soon returned to his heavenly home.

While Christian thought remained under the influence of Plato, it could hardly do otherwise than move ever further in the direction of such a dualistic worldview. Jesus came to be seen not as a human preacher and teacher, but as a divine being from another realm who paid a brief visit to our world. To the extent that this view has held sway in Christian thought and devotion, the original thrust of the language of Incarnation, including what we may here call its secularizing implications, was obscured and lost sight of.

Thus it was not until after Plato's primacy had been challenged by the recovery of Aristotle's philosophy of nature that we find the secularizing process re-emerging. For their knowledge of Aristotle, Christian thinkers were indebted to the Muslim scholars in Spain, who at the same time brought to the Christian West some of the tools of science and the related system of Arabic numerals.

The introduction of Aristotle's natural philosophy led to intellectual ferment in the European universities just then being founded.

It fell to Albertus, followed by Thomas Aquinas, to resolve the theological controversy. This they did by synthesizing the traditional Christian doctrines with Aristotle's philosophy of the natural world, and thereby they furthered the process of secularization.

I suspect Aquinas may have been responsible for inventing the medieval Latin term *supernaturalis*, for he distinguished between natural truth and supernatural truth. Natural truth concerns the natural world, and is arrived at by observation and reasoned speculation. Supernatural truth, however, is beyond human discovery and depends on divine revelation.

SLOUCHING TOWARD MODERNITY

This division of truth into two domains, as we shall see, played a role in the rise of empirical science. Since the Israelite prophets had denied all reality to the nature gods, Christians had shown little interest in the world of nature other than its usefulness in providing sustenance. They saw themselves living in a fallen world, destined for ultimate destruction.

It was St. Francis (1181–1226) who pioneered the reversal of that negative attitude towards nature—not only by treating the birds and animals as his brothers and sisters, but by going so far as to speak of Mother Earth. Not surprisingly, it was from within the order of friars he established that there arose the first proponent of experimental science. This was Roger Bacon (1214–92), who entered into experimental activity with such zeal and energy that he became known everywhere as a kind of wonder worker. He developed the outlines of scientific method, for he believed that by observing a succession of events in nature one could propose a general law to account for them. This he called a "universal experimental principle." Experimentation should then proceed to either verify or falsify that principle.

Yet Roger Bacon was an erratic genius who could also be incredibly naïve, and by later standards his work left much to be desired; nonetheless, it was through his writings that the term "experimental science" became widespread in the West. He strove to create a universal wisdom embracing all the sciences and organized by theology. What is more, it was his deep Christian conviction that spurred him on. Bacon believed that a better understanding of the natural world would serve to confirm the truth of the Christian religion, and this credo was widespread among scientists until well into the nineteenth century.

Thus when Aquinas drew a clear distinction between natural truth and supernatural truth, he unwittingly opened the door for the rise of empirical science. To be sure, this left revealed truth in the superior position; but a philosophy that would undermine the influence of Plato and eventually challenge the concept of supernatural truth was initiated in the following century by another Franciscan, William of Ockham (c. 1300–1349). This vigorous and independent thinker was largely responsible for the spread of a new philosophy known as nominalism.

The prevailing philosophy of the day, based largely on Plato, asserted that only ideas or universal concepts, which are not subject to change and decay, are eternally real. For example, it would have maintained that the idea of a table existed even before the first table had ever been made, and it would continue to exist if all tables were to be destroyed. In direct opposition to this "realist" position, the nominalists contended that the only things that really exist are the particular objects that exemplify the universals. These invisible universals, they said, are nothing more than concepts or names (*nomina*) that have been invented by the human mind after reflecting on the particular objects observed.

GROUND-LEVEL REALITY

Although the great philosophical debate between realism and nominalism may strike us moderns as rather abstract and academic, the opposition between these two ways of understanding the world has had far-reaching consequences. As the nominalists caused attention to be focused more and more on the tangible world and whatever physical forces can be subjected to scientific testing and confirmation, they were nurturing the process of secularization.

This empirical process of thinking led Ockham to assert that humankind can have no reliable knowledge of God other than by divine revelation. He thus drove a wedge between philosophy and theology, and destroyed the Thomistic synthesis. For him theology and philosophy were two quite separate intellectual disciplines. Theology explores and expounds what has been divinely revealed and can be apprehended only by faith. Philosophy explores those aspects of reality that can be examined and understood by human reason and confirmed by empirical means. And philosophy, we must remember, then included physics, which until a hundred years ago was still being called Natural Philosophy in our universities.

Many fourteenth century thinkers began to sense that they were at a crossroads. Nominalism was already being referred to as the *via moderna* in contrast with the *via antiqua*. Thus the teaching of Ockham was recognised in his own day as a serious threat to Christian orthodoxy, and it is not surprising that Ockham was excommunicated from the church and expelled from the Franciscan Order.

In spite of Ockham's fate, nominalism began to capture the foremost minds in the universities of the fourteenth century. It was the forerunner of the Renaissance and the Protestant Reformation, as well as of the innovative philosophy of the seventeenth-century empiricist John Locke. It not only strengthened the foundations of the modern scientific method, but its eventual triumph had the effect of destroying the validity of divine revelation. Frederick Copleston, a twentieth-century Catholic historian of philosophy, deplored the success of nominalism, but rightly said of it, "the way was being prepared for a philosophy of nature which, while not necessarily anti-Christian, emphasized nature as an intelligible totality governed by its own immanent laws."

THE ASCENT OF MAN

The leading figures of the Renaissance are known as the humanists, because they revalued the human condition upwards. Whereas classical Christianity since the time of Augustine had so emphasized the sinful nature of humankind as to conclude that human beings could achieve little without the grace of God, the humanists looked positively on the human situation and gratefully acknowledged the natural ability, initiative, and creativity present in humanity. A vertical fixation on heaven above—the view that characterized the Middle Ages and was symbolized in the great Gothic spires—came to be replaced by the horizontal gaze that acknowledged the beauty of the earth and the worth of human endeavor.

The humanists began to take a keen interest in the physical world. One such was Nicholas of Cusa (c. 1400–1464), who has been described as a model of "the Renaissance Man." Though a cardinal of the church and a theologian, he was also a mathematician, diagnostic physician, experimental scientist, and philosopher. Convinced by his studies of the unity of all reality, he concluded that to know more about God, one must study nature. Such a view encouraged him to urge the increase of knowledge through empirical enquiry. He affirmed that all things are in God and God is in all—a theological position now known as panentheism.

The Renaissance led directly to the Protestant Reformation. I began this series by referring to the great humanist scholar Erasmus and his call for reform, but unfortunately the bitter conflict that broke out between Catholic and Protestant Christians when the Reformation began meant that the ensuing debate was fought out in such theological terms that the humanist movement was overshadowed. Yet it did continue, although strangely enough it was spread more by the works of Shakespeare than by preachers.

But several features of Protestantism resulted in further secularizing. Abolishing the doctrine of Purgatory had the effect of placing more emphasis on everything we do in this world; it meant that death brings us face to face with the Final Judgment, there being no post-mortem opportunity for the purging of our sins. Indeed, Calvin's emphasis on human endeavor in the workplace was so great that some see it as the seedbed of modern capitalism. But the most dramatic step toward secularization was the forcible dissolution of the monasteries, a program that thrust many thousands of monks and nuns out into the world to earn their living.

THE EMERGING TRIUMPH OF REASON

Remembering that empirical science evolved out of philosophy, we may hail as the founding father of British science the philosopher Francis Bacon (1561–1626). He was the first to expound the enterprise of science as a systematic study by which the true scientist amasses data, conducts experiments, and learns the secrets of nature.

It was a body of men inspired by Baconian principles who, in London in 1660, formed the Royal Society—the full title of which is "The Royal Society of London for the Promotion of Natural Knowledge." The composition of this group served to illustrate the still close relationship then existing between science and the Christian tradition, for many of them were clergymen.

For the reasons I have outlined, then, historians, scientists, philosophers, sociologists, and theologians have over the last two hundred years discerned an inherent connection between the modern secular world and Western Christianity.

A few specific examples will serve to illustrate the point. Philosopher and scientist C. F. von Weizsäcker claimed in his Gifford Lectures that the rise of modern science cannot properly be understood or accounted for except against the background of the biblical doctrine of creation, a concept he regarded as "a gift of Christianity to the modern mind." He concluded that "the modern world owes its uncanny success to a great extent to its Christian background," since it is "the result of the secularization of Christianity."

After a lengthy discussion on the origin of modern science in his *Science and the Modern World*, the philosopher A. N. Whitehead announced his conviction that the modern worldview has "but one source for its origin. It must have come from the medieval insistence on the rationality of God, conceived as with the personal energy of Jehovah and with the rationality of a Greek philosopher. . . . the faith in the possibility of science, generated antecedently to the development of modern scientific theory, is an unconscious derivation from medieval theology."

Perhaps the most surprising statement of this sort comes from a group of Anglican scholars who met between 1883–90 to discuss theology at the rectory of J. R. Illingworth. They were convinced that "the epoch in which they lived was one of profound transformation, abounding in new points of view and requiring theology to take a new development." They became known as the *Lux Mundi* (Light of the World) group after the title of the book in which they published their essays. The book went through twelve editions in two years and was still being talked about when I was a student.

Today's Christians may be surprised that as long ago as 1889 these leading theologians were saying, "The last few years have witnessed the gradual acceptance by Christian thinkers of the great scientific generalization of our time—the Theory of Evolution." All of the essays focus on the Christian doctrine of the Incarnation; they set out to see how the affirmation of Jesus as the Light of the World can be reconciled with the new science in general and with the story of biological evolution in particular.

Of course much in the book is now very dated; moreover, it is not easy reading, for these men were well versed in the ancient Fathers, in Aquinas, and in the Reformation thinkers. But consider a couple of small gems from the text. After concluding from his reading of history that "the religion of the incarnation has been the religion of humanity," Illingworth makes this amazing statement: "It is true that secular civilisation has co-operated with Christianity to produce the modern world. Secular civilisation, seen from the Christian viewpoint, is nothing less than the providential correlative and counterpart of the Incarnation." What is more, he said, "Secular thought has so often corrected and counteracted the evil of a Christianity grown professional and false and foul."

Why, then, do the official spokespeople for Christianity so often regard the modern secular world as an enemy to be held at bay? Partly, it would seem, because they have not studied our cultural past sufficiently. Partly, no doubt, because as official dignitaries they have not seen the forest for the trees.

AND THE TRUTH WILL MAKE YOU FREE

An interesting analogy can be seen between the emergence of Christianity out of Judaism and the emergence of the modern secular world out of Christianity. It was not the Jewish priests and scribes who initiated Christianity; they were strongly opposed to it. Christianity came to birth on the margins of Jewish religious life. Jesus, a Galilean Jew, was feared and despised by the politically correct Jerusalem hierarchy, yet he never rejected his Jewish roots. And Paul, though influenced by Greek culture and Stoicism in particular, was a Hellenized Jew who to the end remained proud of his Jewish inheritance.

In like manner it was not the Christian bishops who initiated the modern secular world, but thinkers who stood at the margins of Christian life and practice. Although in their own lifetimes they often found themselves ostracized by Christian orthodoxy, they never saw themselves as in any sense anti-Christian. Among the many pioneers of the modern secular world, some of the most familiar are St. Francis, Roger Bacon, William of Ockham, Martin Luther, Copernicus, Giordano Bruno, Francis Bacon, John Locke, Isaac Newton, David Strauss, and Ludwig Feuerbach.

Further, just as Christianity was not simply the continuation of Judaism but a radical transformation of it, so the modern secular world constitutes the transformation of Christendom into the post-Christian age. And here it should be stressed that post-Christian does not mean anti-Christian, but rather indicates the continuation of the Christian age in a transformed way.

It is of course paradoxical that Christianity should have given birth to the post-Christian secular world. The sociologist Peter Berger drew attention to this when he said, "Christianity has been its own gravedigger." Yet this is no more paradoxical than the theme that lies at the heart of the Christian tradition and is symbolized in the death and resurrection of Jesus Christ: that only out of death comes new life. Christianity came to birth proclaiming the end of the old age and the beginning of the new age. Two thousand years later we are witnessing the rapid decline and death of the triumphant Christendom that resulted from that "new age"—and we observe the arrival of the new, secular, post-Christian age.

Looking back we can trace the Judeo-Christian tradition through several phases of cultural history. The Israelite prophets led it from polytheism to its monotheistic phase. The impact of Jesus of Nazareth produced its incarnational phase. The pioneering Christian thinkers of Second Axial Period have inaugurated its secular phase. Each transition period has had the effect of accelerating cultural change. In crossing over the threshold to the modern secular world we have experienced a further stage of emancipation, being increasingly freed from bondage to external authority and becoming free and autonomous persons. We are now ready to examine in the next lecture the advantages, dangers, and responsibilities brought to us by the advent of the secular age.

12

THE VALUE OF BEING SECULAR

It is sometimes claimed that New Zealand is the most secular country in the Western world. The basis for such a claim is not simply that church-going has reached an all-time low, for that is true of Europe also. It is rather that New Zealand is believed to have extricated itself from its Christian past rather more than any other country shaped by European culture.

Of course the claim is debatable; but if it is true, we may be hard pressed to recognize the values of secularity simply because they are so much a part of our way of life that we take them for granted without recognizing them for what they are. To appreciate the significance of living in a secular society we need to go back two to three hundred years and make a comparison with the Christendom our British ancestors lived in. The whole fabric of European society was then under the spell of Christian authority much more than it is today. Quite understandably, some think that was a preferable state of affairs and would like us to return to it.

ALL THAT GLISTERS IS NOT GOLD

But was classical Christendom quite as wonderful as some imagine? The passage of time can make things appear much more attractive than they were. Certainly there appeared to be less laxity in social life than we observe today to our sorrow. But that is because so little choice of alternative lifestyles existed. The two powerful institutions of Church and state shaped the social *mores* and gave each other mutual support in doing so. And because peer pressure more strongly supported the status quo than it does today, much less latitude was permitted for the personal freedom and individual creativity that people now enjoy. Those who stepped beyond certain clearly defined lines were quickly punished by ostracism, imprisonment, or excommunication. Executions were frequent, and those guilty of lesser crimes were often transported for life to penal colonies like Australia. Making public statements at variance with Christian dogma was regarded as a serious offence, and anything judged to be blasphemy led to harsh punishment.

Consider the example of George Holyoake (1817–1906), who incidentally was a relative of Sir Keith Holyoake, our former prime minister and later Governor-General. At an early age he became attracted to the social ideals of the Scottish reformer Robert Owen. In 1841 he had the odd distinction of being the last person to be imprisoned in Britain on the charge of blasphemy. Holyoake's misdemeanor was this: at the conclusion of a public meeting where the need for social reform was being discussed, this twenty-four year old idealist had the audacity to offer the facetious motion that the General Manager of World Affairs [meaning God] be placed on half-pay for not looking after the poor as he had promised.

A HEALTHY PRAGMATISM

Convicted of blasphemy, Holyoake was sentenced to six months in Gloucester Gaol, and after serving his time coined the term "secularist" to describe his position. He preferred it to the term "atheist," and spent the rest of his life promoting secularism as a replacement for the Christianity he knew. He defined "secularist" as "one who gives primary attention to those subjects the issues of which can be tested by the experience of this life. The secularist principle requires that precedence should be given to the duties of *this life* over those which pertain to another world."

Holyoake was not on the whole opposed to Christianity; rather, he wanted to emancipate daily life from ecclesiastical control so that more could be done to promote social justice and equality of opportunity for all. He drew a clear distinction between religion and morality. "Leave religious dreamers to wait on supernatural aid," he said, "let **us** look to what man can do for man."

The rise of secularism in Britain gave rise to the spread of Freethought Associations in New Zealand—perhaps a major reason for New Zealand's present reputation as the world's most secular country. These Associations flourished between 1870 and 1900, and had their own buildings and Sunday Schools. In the Census of 1881 more than 24,000 registered as freethinkers. One of their leading lights, Robert Stout, was the virtual founder of Victoria University College, Chancellor of the University of New Zealand for twenty years, and Chief Justice from 1899–1927.

The first clear indication that the young New Zealand nation would adopt the secularist policies being advocated by Holyoake is to be found in the 1877 Education Act. This established a national system of primary education that was to be "free, secular and compulsory." What led up to this?

Today we take it for granted that every country should provide a formal education program for its children. But in the nineteenth century the idea that the state should be responsible for education was still quite novel. Such schools as existed in Britain up until the early nineteenth century had been established by the Church, and they were open only to those who could pay for education. That is why in 1780 Robert Raikes founded the institution of the Sunday School. This was originally designed to take the one day of the week when the children of the poor were not working in the factories and use it to teach them to read and write.

LEGISLATING A DREAM

Of course the chief book they were taught to read was the Bible. That was only to be expected, for in those days all education was heavily weighted with church catechisms and biblical knowledge. Entry to the universities of Oxford and Cambridge required a test of religious knowledge and belief, and even then was confined to male members of the Church of England.

This was the background of European migrants to New Zealand from 1840 onwards, and thus it was that the churches established the first schools here also, and they naturally inculcated their children with their own denominational form of Christianity. All children in Otago, for example, had to learn by heart the Westminster Shorter Catechism. But since the migrants came from all parts of the British Isles, New Zealand comprised a more diverse society than the one they had left behind. There soon developed much confusion and religious strife, particularly between Protestants and

Catholics, though even the Protestant denominations were keen to defend their own distinctive beliefs and rituals.

By about 1870 the church-sponsored schools began to seek government aid to meet the needs of a rapidly increasing population. But how was this to be done for such a religiously diverse community? If the state were to take over responsibility for education and the curriculum was to include Christianity, what brand of Christianity was to be taught? With the gift of hindsight we can now say that it was religious diversity, leading often to bitter competition and animosity, that hastened New Zealand's development into a secular state.

The question of religious diversity in New Zealand was resolved in 1877 by deciding that the national education system should be "compulsory, secular and free." Though the churches were not entirely happy with the Act, the Protestants somewhat reluctantly accepted it, mainly to prevent the state from subsidizing what they judged to be the evil of Popery. The Protestant churches were confident they could provide their children with a religious education through the institution of the Sunday School, since by then it no longer had to teach children to read and write. The Roman Catholic Church, unwilling to allow the educational curriculum to be fragmented into religious and secular, took on the heavy financial burden of providing a complete educational system for its own people.

THE PAYOFF: SOCIAL STABILITY

The 1877 Education Act did more than simply avoid religious dissension; it began to shape the secular character of New Zealand society. Through the way it chose to educate the vast majority of its young people, it laid the foundation for a modern secular state.

Of course New Zealand still shows many of the signs of its Christian past, for the British migrants brought many Christian customs with them. Parliament opens with prayer. In the law courts the oath is taken on the Bible. For a long time Sunday was strictly observed as a day of rest, and is still different from other days.

The Christian holy days remain as holidays. But there is no state church as in England and Scotland—even though the Anglican Church, being the largest, has shown a tendency to assume that role. The churches can no longer dictate to the state on religious and moral issues. Their status has been reduced to that of being lobby-groups and even that power has declined markedly with the passing years.

Even though New Zealand was tacitly judged to be a Christian country in the nineteenth century, it is no longer so in the twenty-first. It is best described as a secular country with a Christian cultural heritage. Indeed, the most important aspect of that heritage is found in the values we commonly share. These are often referred to as Christian values, though in the form in which they are expressed some of them are less than 300 years old. Perhaps more than that of any other country, our history over the last 150 years demonstrates how a post-Christian secular society can evolve out of a specifically Christian society without any noticeable social revolution.

While I contend that it is our responsibility to keep New Zealand secular because of the values intrinsic to a secular society, I must repeat from the first lecture what I mean by the word "secular." A secular society is oriented to "this-world" and not towards an unseen "other-world." A secular society is guided by natural and humanistic ideals and not by supposedly supernatural ones received by revelation from a higher realm.

The inherent values of such a secular society derive from the fact that the structure of the state is religiously neutral. A secular state does not identify with any particular religion or ideology. It neither promotes nor defends any particular religious stance, but neither does it attempt to stamp religion out. A truly secular state allows its citizens maximum personal freedom; the only human behavior it should forcibly prevent is that which is harmful to other citizens. A secular society is fully democratic in that it is ruled by all of its citizens collectively and not by any form of dictatorship, whether human or divine. A secular state is the precise opposite of a theocracy.

A COCKEYED OPTIMIST . . .

This was the burden of the philosopher John Stuart Mill (1806–73) when in 1859 he published his famous essay *On Liberty*. It has been called "the first modern exposition of a theory of a secular state." He called for an open society that allowed wide disagreements, contending that only with the interplay of conflicting ideas is truth free to emerge. Mill, like all democrats, assumed we are all potentially wise and capable of making a good decision.

He may have been overconfident about the human condition; indeed, his ideal secular society may not be wholly achievable. Yet it remains the ideal we should be ever seeking to attain. And we should rejoice in those elements of it that we have already implemented here in New Zealand, circumstances that were not present in the Christendom of more than two hundred years ago.

. . . JUSTIFIED BY THE RESULTS

The first value of living in a secular state is simply personal freedom—the freedom to think for oneself, without having beliefs imposed by an external source, whether that be the state or an anthology of sacred writings from the past. The freedom to think outside the square nurtures our inherent creativity. Next comes the freedom to express one's thoughts without fear of reprisal. A secular state defends the freedom of the public media to transmit information, provided only that it conforms to the truth.

Personal freedom to think and follow one's inclinations also implies freedom of religion—the freedom to determine and explore whatever form of religious belief and practice one finds most satisfying. As Robert Stout once addressed the churches on behalf of freethinkers, "We shall not attack you or try to exterminate you. We shall simply *explain* you in the context of the now developing science of comparative religion."

The second value of living in a secular state is its discernment and defense of human rights. Classical Christendom never acknowledged human rights. Traditional Christianity focused not on human rights, but on human responsibilities—responsibilities to God, to King and country, and to one's fellows. All of these were believed to be encoded in the Bible, and that explains why the absolute monarch of former times could appeal to the "divine right of kings."

Of course one might argue that if only Christians had in all things followed the Golden Rule and loved their neighbors as themselves, then spelling out human rights would not have become necessary. But they did not, and so it did become necessary. And for that reason it is now the task of the secular state not only to protect its citizens from external threats, but to safeguard their human rights from threats within the state.

The third value of the secular state is the welcome it provides for diversity. The tolerance that Christians once regarded as a weakness has now become a virtue. Under the rule of king and Church everyone was expected to conform to the norm long established by tradition and divine authority. Indeed, until quite recently those in England who did not belong to the Church of England were labelled non-conformists, and those who strayed too far from the norm were not tolerated. A secular society, by contrast, sets a positive value on diversity and does not expect all of its citizens to be clones of some ideal model. Of course the secular society must still set some limits to human behavior. This follows from its duty to safeguard the human rights of its citizens, and therefore behavior detrimental to the welfare of others cannot be tolerated. But having noted that caveat, we can boast that the secular state allows much more latitude to human behavior than closed societies do.

So it is that only with the progressive secularization of society have we advanced by degrees towards a purer democracy, abolished slavery, promoted the emancipation of women, curbed the evils of racism, and accepted the legitimacy of homosexuality. It is a sad commentary on Christendom that the church was initially opposed to every one of these marks of a secular society.

The advent of secularism has gradually emancipated us from whatever in our cultural past promoted depersonalization and stereotyping: we have learned to condemn cultural conditioning, class stratification, and discrimination on the basis of race, color, sex, and age. People are being freed and encouraged to develop their human worth and potential in whatever way best fulfills the physical, intellectual, and spiritual dimensions of the human condition.

ONE SHINING VISION

A magnificent but heart-rending illustration of this process of emancipation is to be found in the life story of Ayaan Hirsi Ali, the young Somali woman who was named by *Time* Magazine as one of the 100 Most Influential People of 2005. Her book entitled *Infidel* is an account of her struggle against great odds to become a fully emancipated, responsible, and self-fulfilling person.

Hirsi Ali was raised in a strict Muslim family that in turn was part of a closely-knit Somali clan. Among the many sufferings and privations stemming from the Somali civil war, she was subjected to female circumcision and brutal beatings. In her adolescence she became a devout believer under the influence of the newly established Muslim Brotherhood, but to escape from an enforced marriage she sought refugee status in Holland, where her outstanding abilities led to increasingly responsible roles. University studies in Political Science led to an appreciation of what the Enlightenment had done for Western society and opened her eyes to new social and religious possibilities. Assuming a leadership role among her fellow Islamic refugees, she began to fight for women's rights and the reform of Islam. This led her into the political arena, and she was elected to the Dutch Parliament.

Gradually and very reluctantly she came to realize how oppressive had been the Islamic culture of Somalia in which she was reared. In 2003 she met a Dutch TV journalist named Theo van Gogh with whom she produced a ten-minute documentary film entitled *Submission: Part One.* It was a plea for the reform of Islam in the form of questions addressed to Allah. That documentary brought to a head the Islamic reaction that had been steadily growing against her. In 2004 Theo van Gogh was stabbed to death by Islamic extremists and Ayaan Ali, being a Member of Parliament, was sequestered under police protection. This tragic series of events led to the fall of the Dutch Government, and Ayaan Ali found it necessary to seek safety in the United States.

This is not simply the story of how an inquisitive and intelligent little girl progressed from a dutiful and submissive daughter to a pioneer for women's rights and social reform. It is also a parable that epitomizes a phenomenon occurring today on the grand scale—the pain and anguish accompanying the birth-pangs of a global secular society. While some rejoice in it because they see it as the emancipation of people from the stranglehold of religion, others deplore and violently oppose it. They see secularization as a force that undermines the religion that gave their culture cohesion, and one that results in the decline of moral standards and the slow slide into social chaos.

TWO KINDS OF BLINDNESS

The story of Ayaan Hirsi Ali all too vividly attests that any truly secular society will have enemies. They are of two opposing kinds. At the one extreme are the religious fundamentalists who, whether Christian or Muslim, want to re-impose their beliefs and practices on what they see as a fallen world. At the other extreme are the militant ideologues who want to curtail and at last stamp out all forms of traditional religion and establish a uniformly atheistic society.

It was this latter extreme that the philosopher Karl Popper brought to our attention in 1945 when he published *The Open Society and its Enemies*. It is interesting to note that he wrote this book while lecturing in philosophy at Canterbury University, having come to New Zealand from Vienna as a Jewish refugee to escape from Nazi Germany. What I am calling the secular society is pretty much what Popper meant by the Open Society. The enemies he referred to were, of course, the totalitarian juggernauts of Nazism and Communism.

Soviet Russia under communist rule was not a secular state for the simple reason that it was not religiously neutral. It was an anti-religious state that made atheism a dogma to be imposed on all. It did not leave its citizens free to follow their own religious preferences.

Contrast Soviet Russia with India. Even though the Indian people are intensely religious, often in fairly traditional ways, the state of India that came to birth in 1947 declared itself in its very constitution to be a secular state. Being secular, the state of India leaves its citizens free to be Hindu, Muslim, Sikh, Jain, or atheist just as they prefer. It neither imposes one religion exclusively nor does it seek to stamp out religion.

New Zealand has become a secular state not by constitution but by cultural evolution. But we should not take this development for granted simply because it has been natural and relatively peaceful. Even in New Zealand the two extreme enemies of the secular society are still present. There are some who would like New Zealand to revert to the kind of Christian society that existed in the days of Christendom. The Destiny Church, for example, has clearly indicated its political intentions in this respect.

On the other hand, it is just because of the 1877 Education Act that we face the danger of going in the opposite direction. By stating that no teaching of religion should take place in our schools it has led us to interpret the word secular to mean non-religious or even anti-religious. It should, of course, be understood to mean religiously neutral.

This fact began to become a little clearer with the recent resurgence of Maori culture. The majority of pakeha seem to have little awareness that they have a culture, let alone any knowledgeable appreciation of it. The reason for this is that our national educational system tends to leave New Zealanders ignorant of their cultural past, so largely shaped by Christianity. It is important for us, then, not to allow either of these two extreme positions to undermine the religious neutrality of our secular society.

I became aware of these two opposing forces in New Zealand because of an incident that occurred some thirty-five years ago. The Department of Education judged the time ripe for a review of the secular clause in the 1877 Education Act. Since the ecclesiastical rivalry that led to the inclusion of this clause had long since been amicably resolved, it was thought that the study of religion could be re-introduced into the curriculum to enable each generation to gain a more complete understanding of our cultural past. To this end the Department organized a conference in Christchurch to which it invited such interested parties as teachers, parents, and the Council for Christian Education.

For this conference I was invited to prepare a broad-ranging paper that I entitled "The Religious Content of a Liberal Education in a Secular World." After defining religion in broad terms, I stressed its importance for a well-rounded curriculum that aimed to prepare young people for life and offered some proposals for how this could be done.

AN UNFORTUNATE STALEMATE

My suggestions largely followed the example of Britain, where religious studies had become a compulsory subject. But such a venture for New Zealand was finally stymied by two extremist groups at the conference: conservative Christians insisted that traditional Christianity alone should be taught, and the militant secularists refused to allow any mention of religion in the official school curriculum. This temporary and cruelly ironic alliance of two extreme groups cost New Zealand an opportunity to develop a form of education that could have promoted tolerance, understanding, and goodwill in our increasingly pluralist society.

The result has been that a sort of religious or spiritual vacuum now exists in New Zealand. While Maoridom revives its own forms of spirituality, and while the more traditional forms of religion cater to a minority of the non-Maori society, the majority of New Zealanders have been left with little knowledge of our past spiritualities and have been given no guidance as to how to develop their own.

Now let us turn to the world scene, where the problems preventing the emergence of a global secular society are much greater. Not only is the process of secularization much less advanced in some countries than in others, but its enemies are much more powerful. Secularization is most advanced in the Christian world simply because that is where it emerged, and primarily for that reason the non-Christian world often regards it as a foreign influence that must be resisted. Resistance is particularly strong in the Islamic world, and especially in Iran and Pakistan, which were specifically designed to be Islamic states. In Turkey, by contrast, Kemal Ataturk carried through a major cultural revolution in 1922 that left his country much more secularized than before. Egypt, largely due to the long British influence there, is also more secularized.

CHALLENGES TO FREEDOM

Around the globe today, the chief enemies of the secular state are the growing forces of religious fundamentalism. They arose in the twentieth century as a reaction to the spread of secularization in both the Christian and the Islamic worlds. Ironically, each of these fundamentalisms grew out of a movement that was healthy and positive.

We are more familiar with the way it arose in the Christian world. The Protestant Reformers of the sixteenth century set out to reform the church, and by the eighteenth century, no longer restrained by papal authority, Protestant thinkers gave rise to the Enlightenment. This in turn hastened the arrival of liberalism, Christian Modernism, and secularization. At the beginning of the twentieth century fundamentalism arose as a reactionary force, seeking to counter liberalism and stamp out secularism, and Christian fundamentalism has been growing ever since.

Strangely parallel to this is the rise of Islamic fundamentalism. It began in the eighteenth century with the Saudi Arabian Wahhabi movement, which sought the purification of Islam. Then the influence of the Western Enlightenment gave rise in the late nineteenth century to a form of Modernism that was more successfully crushed in the Islamic world than in the Christian simply because it was seen as foreign. The success of the Wahhabi movement inspired the foundation of the Muslim Brotherhood in Egypt in 1928, a group that sought not only to revive traditional Islam and restore theocracy to the Islamic world, but also to root out what it saw as the insidious effects of Western secularization. A direct link connects the Egyptian Muslim Brotherhood to Al Qaeda in Saudi Arabia.

Religious fundamentalism, whether Christian or Muslim, rejects the human freedoms that grew out of the Western Enlightenment and is dedicated to the elimination of secular humanism. Fundamentalism asserts that humans must submit to the authority of the Divine Being, whose revealed truths and absolute commands they believe to have been permanently revealed— in the Torah for the Jew, in the Bible for the Christian, and in the Qur'an for the Muslim.

Fundamentalism is distrustful of human reason. It cannot enter into open dialogue because its dogmas must not be questioned. It is wary of democracy, the assertion of human rights, and the equality of the sexes. It favors strong, male, charismatic leadership, both in religion and in society.

Fundamentalism seeks to exercise control over others by establishing theocratic societies that conform to the absolutes it believes to have been divinely revealed. Hence Israel *must* be a Jewish state, Iran *must* be an Islamic state, while American fundamentalists *insist on* making the United States a more truly Christian state.

The widespread tension and unrest in the Middle East is admittedly complex and many-faceted, inasmuch as it includes such issues as competition for oil and the resurgence of nationalism. Yet the common factor that underlies the whole poisonous admixture is the rise of fundamentalism. President George Bush and his supporters made a great mistake in treating the Iraq war as a war against terrorism. Terrorism is simply one of the unfortunate symptoms of a conflict that has much deeper roots. Above all else, it reflects a "clash of fundamentalisms", as Tariq Ali showed in his book of that name.

WHEN IGNORANT ARMIES CLASH BY NIGHT

The Jewish fundamentalists who hold the balance of power in any Israeli government insist that the whole of the Holy Land belongs to the Jewish people by divine right. They stand in the way of any plan to establish a just settlement for the Palestinians. The now long-standing Israeli-Palestinian conflict is in some respects the key to the whole of the Middle East unrest.

Muslim fundamentalists see the establishment of the state of Israel as an unjustified invasion of the Islamic world and they hope to destroy it. Failure to do so has exacerbated Muslim discontent with the secularized Christian West, which Muslim fundamentalists now regard as the domain of Satan. The Qur'anic concept of *jihad* (meaning "striving") is motivating Muslim fundamentalists to strive to eliminate all Western influence and power over them and to restore the Islamic world to its former greatness by establishing truly Islamic states after the pattern of Iran and Pakistan. All who die in this holy war are judged to be martyrs; suicide bombers expect to go straight to their reward in heaven.

The Christian fundamentalists who help to keep Bush in power see the Islamic fundamentalists as an axis of evil, the struggle against which they consider a God-given task. What is even worse, the Christian fundamentalists of America secretly hope the Middle East conflict will lead to the cosmic battle of Armageddon that will hasten the return of the Lord Jesus Christ.

In Iraq today we witness not only a clash between the Islamic fundamentalists and Christian fundamentalists, but the revival of the long-standing conflict within Islam between the Sunnis and the Shi'ites. Saddam Hussein, the leader of the secular Ba'ath party had suppressed that conflict, but only by cruelly oppressive means. Now, American intervention has brought it out into the open, and any hope of seeing Iraq evolve into a true democracy is doomed for the foreseeable future. For democracy and secularity go hand in hand; and fundamentalism, whether Muslim or Christian, springs from its inherent opposition to secularization.

IT TAKES A (GLOBAL) VILLAGE

Not only is the secular state difficult to bring to birth, but even when achieved its maintenance requires continued effort. Where personal freedom is not matched equally with personal responsibility, the secular society begins to erode. So even we who enjoy the benefits of a secular society can become its enemies if we do not both learn to appreciate what we have and work hard to maintain it.

If we fail to do this, the secular society, instead of manifesting an harmonious and co-operative spirit, descends by degrees into a collection of greedy and self-centered individualists among whom anti-social and even violent behavior becomes more prevalent. This turmoil produces outcries to bring back the birch, institute longer terms of imprisonment, and restore capital punishment. When such right-wing reaction gains sufficient strength, people will either grudgingly or willingly submit themselves to a military dictatorship that promises law and order. And then, of course, the secularizing process has to start all over again.

To maintain a healthy secular state we need to nurture personal responsibility. That requires some form of spirituality, as it did in the religious societies of the past. But what form of spirituality is possible in a secular world? That is the issue we shall turn to next.

13

SPIRITUALITY IN THE SECULAR WORLD

The first century to feel the impact of secularization was the nineteenth. Not surprisingly, therefore, the Cambridge historian Owen Chadwick entitled his Gifford Lectures of 1975 *The Secularization of the European Mind in the Nineteenth Century*. Even though vast numbers of people were so unaware of the cultural change going on around them that the churches remained full until the end of the century, many academic minds were busy exploring the new possibilities that the eighteenth-century Enlightenment had opened up for them.

This prompted Pope Pius IX to attempt to counter the secularizing process by issuing his now notorious Syllabus of Errors in 1864. Here are some of the 80 beliefs he condemned as erroneous:

- All the truths of religion proceed from the innate strength of human reason; hence reason is the ultimate standard by which man can and ought to arrive at every kind of truth.
- Every man is free to embrace and profess whatever religion he shall, guided by the light of reason, consider true.
- Moral laws do not stand in need of the divine sanction.
- The Roman Pontiff can and ought to reconcile himself with progress, liberalism, and modern civilization.

A SCANDALOUS SEMINARIAN

But in that same year, 1864, a French Catholic scholar, Ernest Renan (1823–92) published a book that shocked the Catholic world. While training for the priesthood at a prestigious seminary in Paris, he studied the *Life of Jesus Critically Examined*, published by the German scholar David Strauss in 1835. This book sowed in his mind seeds of doubt about the truth of Christianity. Accordingly, rather than accept ordination, he became a free-lance writer, and so quickly gained a reputation as a scholar that the French Emperor sent him on an archaeological expedition to Palestine and Syria. The result was the first modern book about Jesus to be written by a scholar who had taken the trouble to walk around Galilee.

In this book, *The Life of Jesus,* Renan brought Jesus back to earth from the heavenly places to which Christian belief had long exalted him. He portrayed a wholly human Jesus in his natural setting, stripping the divine Christ of all the supernatural elements surrounding him in the Gospel stories. The book went through eight editions in three months and completely scandalized conventional Christians.

Modern scholars do not think highly of the book, for they doubt that we possess sufficient historical material to reconstruct Jesus' life. According to the scholars of the Jesus Seminar, for example, the best that we can do is to recover the "voiceprints and footprints" of the historical Jesus. Renan, however, used his fertile imagination to fill in the gaps, and portrayed Jesus as a charming preacher leisurely wandering round Galilee. Albert Schweitzer said rather scathingly of Renan's rendering, "The gentle Jesus, the beautiful Mary, the fair Galileans who formed the retinue of the 'amiable carpenter' might have been taken over from the shop-window of an ecclesiastical art shop in Paris." Yet even Schweitzer conceded that the book had a magic about it, so much so that it "marked an epoch, not for the Catholic world only, but for general literature." The die had been cast for the acceptance of a completely human Jesus.

Since the time of Strauss and Renan, Christian scholars and preachers have focused increasingly on the humanity of Jesus and ever less on his divinity. Seeing Jesus as a Galilean teacher meant, of course, that he was being secularized—that is, brought back into this world. Hymns began to appear that celebrated him not as a divine Savior, but as a hero who led an exemplary life. This trend continued, particularly in the latter half of the twentieth century. Yet from its inception this humanization of Jesus was rejected and often condemned by those of a conservative or orthodox persuasion.

THE END OF RELIGION?

When Renan was appointed to the chair of Hebrew at the Collège de France in 1862, he referred to Jesus in his inaugural lecture as "an incomparable man." In his eyes that was the highest praise that one could bestow, but the uproar that resulted from those words led to his suspension from the chair, and it was not restored to him until 1870. In 1868 he wrote, "Whether one is pleased or not, the supernatural is disappearing from the world: only people not of this age have faith in it. Does this mean that religion must crash simultaneously? Indeed not. Religion is necessary. The day when it disappears the very heart of humanity will dry up. Religion is as eternal as poetry, as love. It will survive the demolition of all illusions . . . Under some form or other, faith will express the transcendent value of life."

A few years earlier, Ludwig Feuerbach had similarly assigned to religion the place of highest importance in human culture, even though he judged it to be the product of human beings and not the result of a divine revelation. He believed that more than anything else religion distinguishes the human species from other animals. He judged it to be essential, for in religion we come to terms with our finiteness and find our true place in the natural scheme of things.

Neither Feuerbach nor Renan regarded supernatural beliefs to be an essential element of religion. Unfortunately, many who today champion the secular world persist in that assumption and consequently have a negative attitude toward the very word "religion." This is the reason why Dietrich Bonhoeffer said, "We are moving towards a completely religionless time; people as they are now simply cannot be religious any more." Though as I pointed out in the first lecture it is possible to define religion in a way that does not involve the supernatural, I choose here to use the word "spirituality"—a term with which many people feel more comfortable—to avoid unnecessary confusion.

But even the term "spirituality" presents some problems. Because it belongs to the family of words derived from "spirit," it has close associations with the supernatural worldview that is being left behind. In the ancient Roman world *spiritus* meant "breath," "air," or "wind"—and hence came to refer to any such vital human quality as courage and dignity. Because air, breath, and wind could not be seen, spirit was conceived as a form of invisible life-giving energy; and to the world of spirit belonged gods, angels, and other unseen beings. Thus the Bible declares that "God is spirit." Humans conceived of themselves as having bodies like the animals, but possessing souls that belonged to the realm of spirit.

The scientists of the seventeenth century unintentionally undermined the reality of that supposed spirit world when they showed that the air we breathe is a gas that is just as physical as solids and liquids. In other words, they secularized the traditional world of spirit. Only slowly has it dawned upon us that in talking about spirit we are talking about something far less substantial than a gas—whether that gas be air, breath, or wind. Indeed, spirit has now lost its "substance" referent altogether, and has become a purely abstract term, a frozen metaphor from a now obsolete worldview. For that reason even the terminology of spirit and spirituality has become somewhat problematical. The only way these words can have meaning in the secular world is to understand them as metaphoric, symbolic, or poetic.

RELIGION AS POETRY

But that brings us back to the words of Renan: "Religion is as eternal as poetry." Today even theologians are saying that God-talk has more in common with poetry than with science. Religious thought and feeling are often most adequately expressed and effectively communicated in the poetry of hymns and liturgical readings. One of the fifteenth century Popes claimed that Luther had sung his people into heresy. Today's ready acceptance of the poetic nature of spiritual terminology is more common outside of traditionally religious circles than within them, and largely because traditional religion has been too committed to an outmoded interpretation of the spiritual.

Take for example the word soul. Though many no longer regard the human soul as a self-contained and immortal spiritual entity in the way our forbears did, we may say of a musician that he is technically skillful but shows no soul in his playing. Similarly, we may judge some dramatic production to be a very spirited performance.

Whenever we feel drawn to make some reference to the human spirit we are referring to a dimension of human existence, yet one that is other than emotion, volition, and cognition, though dependent upon all three. This spiritual dimension of human existence is expressed most powerfully in the arts.

If we explore the human spirit a little further, we find that it is closely associated with the highest values or qualities we associate with the state of being a person. This is why in Galatians 5:22 these qualities are referred to as gifts of the spirit, and enumerated as love, joy, peace, patience, kindness, goodness, faithfulness, gentleness, and self-control.

These qualities, we should note, cannot be labelled intellectual. They cannot even be called moral virtues, though some of them certainly have moral implications. One has a moral obligation to be honest, for example, but does one have a moral obligation to be patient or gentle? These so-called spiritual qualities are associated with what we regard as the highest manifestation of human behavior, and the highest level of self-conscious human existence to which we can aspire. Some of these spiritual qualities point primarily to the quality of life experienced within the person (such as joy or self-control), while others refer to the quality of our personal relationships with others (such as kindness, love, faithfulness, and gentleness).

WORLDLY SPIRITUALITY

Thus far I have been explaining how traditionally religious terms such as "spirit" and "spiritual" continue to be used in a secular age. Insofar as they are in complete harmony with the secular world we can say they have been secularized.

The word "spirituality" has a two-fold use. On the one hand it can refer to the spiritual dimension of the human condition, while on the other it can characterize the particular practices in which that dimension is both manifested and nurtured. Of course these two usages share an essential relationship of the kind that should always exist between theory and practice. This can be clearly illustrated by looking at the spirituality of two great religious traditions.

The essence of Islam is human submission to the omnipotent deity, Allah, the only true God, who is believed to have revealed his will in the Qur'an. That is the theoretical substance of Muslim spirituality. In terms of practice, however, the substance of Muslim spirituality is a threefold obligation: five times a day devout Muslims prostrate themselves in both bodily and mental submission to Allah, facing Mecca, the geographical place where the divine revelation took place. At least once in a lifetime the Muslim tries to make the pilgrimage to Mecca. Muslims study and memorize the words of Qur'an, thus immersing their minds in what for them is the revealed will of Allah.

Buddhist spirituality is noticeably different. Its theoretical substance is the acknowledgment of the Buddha's analysis of the human condition; this affirms the universality of suffering, the wheel of continual rebirth, and the possibility of gaining release from rebirth by becoming enlightened. But the practice of Buddhist spirituality calls for actively embracing the Three Jewels—the Buddha, the Dharma, and the Sangha—and following of the eight-fold path that leads to Enlightenment. This latter takes the form of meditation, the clearing of the mind, the release of the will from desire, and the abandonment of possessions—which together lead to the release from suffering. In each of the great religious traditions the basic form of spirituality expresses and rehearses those things that give identity to that culture.

NEW WINE AND OLD SKINS

With the advent of the secular age it became clear that certain aspects of past spiritualities, particularly those of the monotheistic traditions, must be abandoned. For example, their authoritarianism, their exclusivism (that is, their insistence that theirs is the only way), their patriarchal character, their other-worldliness, their sexism, their slave mentality, and their denigration of individuality.

But what are we left with? What can one discover in secular culture that can lead to some appropriate form of spirituality? As we have seen, secular culture does provide us with values, one of which is personal freedom. But this value in itself means we are free to find or to create our own most satisfying form of spirituality. In the secular age, therefore, there cannot be only one uniform type of spirituality. Even though that may have been the ideal in the past, the secular society is sufficiently open to allow a multiplicity of spiritualities.

That in fact is the direction in which we have been moving for some time. First of all, each of the world religions has already produced not just one uniform spirituality, but a whole family of spiritualities. We have been long used to that in the Christian world because the Protestant Reformation opened the door for an ever-increasing multiplication of denominations and sects. In the twentieth century that process virtually exploded. Scholars who specialize in the subject have reported that 1100 new religions emerged in South Africa during that century, and Japan has produced 700 new religions since World War II! Some of these new religions clearly reveal their Christian or Buddhist roots, while others have lost all visible connection with the past. In short, the secular age has not only privatized religion and spirituality, but has generated a vast smorgasbord of spiritualities from which one can choose.

ALL ROADS LEAD TO HOME . . .

But with all their diversity, do they have a common thread that indicates their rootedness in the secular age? A useful suggestion that may help us to know what to look for is provided by the Jewish philosopher Martin Buber in his great spiritual classic *I and Thou*. There he maintained that to regain an adequate understanding of spirituality in the modern secular world, we must turn to the subject of personal relationships. It is a mistake, in his view, for us to think of spirit as some intangible thing within us. "Spirit is not in the I but between I and You," he said. "Spirit is not like the blood that circulates in you but like the air in which you breathe." Note that Buber was recovering something of the original meaning of the word "spirit," yet he was using the word metaphorically to refer to that indefinable something that brings cohesion and quality to the life of a society, something that emerges from the way we relate to another at a personal level.

What is more, it was by directing our attention to the essential importance of human relationships that Buber found he could point to the reality of God. Since God is not a self-existing and objective being, then God can neither be seen nor described. Indeed, God cannot even be talked about, said Buber. God is pure subject and therefore can only be addressed. We address God whenever we address or enter into communion with a fellow human being. God is the spirit present wherever three or more are gathered in a real community. In effect, Buber was secularizing God-talk in much the same way as Renan had secularized Jesus.

This secularizing process can be appreciated even more fully if we trace the spirituality of our Christian past back to its roots. When we observe the great variety of present-day Christian spiritualities— all the way from the elevated liturgy of Catholicism's High Mass to the hand clapping and speaking in tongues of Pentecostalism to the silent meditation of a Quaker Meeting—we should be asking what it is they have in common. The answer can be easily overlooked because it is so obvious, so simple, and so secular.

. . . AND HOME IS WHERE THE HEART IS

In each case there is a coming together of people to celebrate that which is of greatest importance to them. Let me repeat that: a coming together to celebrate that which is of greatest importance to them. We in the West are so used to associating this simple coming together with religious practice that we often assume it applies to all religions. That is not so. It applies chiefly to those, such as Jews, Christians, Muslims, Sikhs, whose traditions can be traced back to Judaism. Because it was not a universal practice, we even miss the significance of the simple words in Acts about the first Christians— "All who had faith *came together* and they *had all things in common* and day by day they *went to the temple together* and they *had meals together* in their homes." In coming together they were nurturing their personal relationships with one another and becoming a fellowship, a community.

This coming together did not originate with the Christians; they were simply continuing the Jewish form of spirituality that had been slowly evolving for some four to five hundred years. The Jews called it the Synagogue—a Greek word that simply means "a coming together." After the fall of the Davidic Kingdom and the destruction of the Temple, the institution of the synagogue evolved slowly and naturally as Jews came together to give one another mutual support in their distress. They did this by recalling their cultural past and encoding it in a set of Scriptures so they would never lose their identity.

The synagogue was not a sacred institution like the Temple. Priests exercised no role within it. The synagogue was essentially a layman's institute, a very secular institution by comparison with the temples of the day, and it was democratically self-ruling. A non-Jewish scholar has referred to it as Judaism's greatest gift to humankind. The synagogue became the prototype of the Christian church, the Islamic mosque, and the Sikh Gurdwara.

When the first Christians came together to remember and celebrate the impact Jesus had made on them, they were establishing a Christian synagogue. It is largely due to an odd linguistic fact that the early Christian congregations were not called synagogues. The first Christians, being Jews, took as their Scriptures the Jewish Bible, what we call the Old Testament. But by that time Greek had become the common language of the Eastern Mediterranean world and most Jews were reading from a Greek translation, and therefore our earliest Christian records are in Greek. The two Greek words used to translate the Hebrew for "congregation" and "assembly" were *synagoge* and *ekklesia*. Soon, however, Jews and Christians became mutually exclusive, and since Jews had already laid claim to the word "synagogue," Christians adopted the word "ecclesia," or church.

Even so, the Christian churches still resembled Jewish synagogues much more than the hierarchical institutions they later became. They were not ruled or ministered to by priests, but were fellowships of lay people. This was acknowledged much later by the Protestant Reformers when they tried to replace the priesthood with an order of ministry, and later again by the Plymouth Brethren, who in the nineteenth century abandoned even an ordained ministry.

AN ANCIENT STRATEGY . . .

And what was the primary spiritual practice that took place in the Christian churches? Then as down to the present day, in most of the ecclesiastical streams into which classical Christianity has now become divided, the central celebration of spirituality was what Christians variously call the Mass, Holy Communion, the Eucharist, or the Lord's Supper. If we trace this back to its point of origin, we may be surprised to find what a secular or this-worldly origin it had.

The Christian Eucharist did not originate with Jesus and the Last Supper: behind it was the Jewish Kiddush—a simple sharing of bread and wine that concluded the meeting together at the synagogue. It had nothing of the exclusivity that later became an element of the Christian Eucharist, for it constituted a commemoration of the tradition that held them together; in fact, the bread was often taken to symbolize the manna with which their ancestors were sustained while wandering in the wilderness. But the kiddush also had the effect of cementing the bonds of personal relationship to one another as well as to their spiritual ancestors.

And how did the Kiddush arise? It was taken into the synagogue from the family setting: the bonds that hold a family together are regularly strengthened by the sharing of meals. The kiddush was thus nurturing a value that had come to be highly prized among the ancient Semitic people, one that has been preserved almost unchanged among the Bedouin to this day.

The ancient Semites, living as they did in the often hostile and sometimes uninhabitable desert, came to prize hospitality above all things. Hospitality was the key to survival in an unfriendly world. So one was bound to provide hospitality—not only to the stranger, but even to one's enemies. On the one hand, nothing could be more secular and down to earth than inviting strangers to share one's meal. On the other hand it was regarded as a sacred duty.

. . . IN A MODERN SETTING

In stripping away the supernatural trappings with which the later forms of Christian spirituality were clothed, and by tracing them back to their primitive roots, we find ourselves in the same secular world that we inhabit. They lived in a world that transcended them. Just as their spirituality grew out of the necessity to respond to that which transcended them by threatening their existence, so it is with us. Simply because we in the modern secular world have achieved a degree of personal freedom that could not have been dreamed of in earlier centuries, that does not mean the end of our experience of transcendence, of what came to be symbolized by the notion of God.

What transcends us today, however, is not some imagined supernatural reality but—as it was for our ancient ancestors—simply nature itself. Even such a simple and this-worldly phenomenon as the climate transcends us. We talk about it every day, and even try to predict it, but it eludes our attempts to master it. In fact, in our very ignorance we may have brought about changes that will make our climate increasingly more threatening.

The immensity of space transcends us: the very size of the universe is mind-boggling. The passing of time also transcends us: we cannot speed it up or slow it down. The future arrives irrespective of what we do, and we know not for sure what a day may bring forth. However much we learn through science about nature and the way it works, this universe of space and time completely transcends us, filling us with awe and wonder. And this shows how the experience of transcendence has been secularized.

The modern study of ecology is helping us to understand the awe-inspiring way in which all life on this planet forms a complex, interdependent whole. All living creatures are complex systems made up of such components as carbon, hydrogen, nitrogen, and oxygen—which are themselves lifeless. And not only does each living organism constitute a self-contained living system, but together with its environment it forms a larger living system that could be called a "life field," or ecosystem.

The earth has provided certain basic conditions that must be met by all earthly creatures if they are to survive as a species. Like all other species, humans have evolved within those parameters. For humans to be healthy they must be able to breathe fresh air, drink clean water, eat an adequate amount of nourishing food, and live in an environment not too different from that in which they became human. The more the environment changes from that in which a species has evolved, the more the health and behavior of that species will show maladjustment; and if such changes are too great or prolonged, then its health will deteriorate and it will die out. A full appreciation of the whole ecosystem has led some to describe the earth itself in terms of an organism. The biosphere is the living skin of the earth in the same way as bark is the living skin of a tree.

BACK TO BASICS

So it is that this-worldly needs of pure air, clean water, healthy food, adequate shelter, the regeneration of the species, and the overcoming of threats to human survival have become the genuinely "religious" issues to which we must "devote" ourselves—together, of course, with the age-old issues of learning how to live together in justice and harmony. In spite of all of our modern sophistication, scientific knowledge, technological expertise, philosophical wisdom, and traditional forms of spirituality, it is in response to these issues that the new forms of spirituality will arise.

It was a Catholic priest, Thomas Berry, who said "We must move beyond a spirituality focused simply on the divine and the human to a spirituality concerned with survival of the natural world in its full splendor, its fertility, and its integral well-being as the larger spiritual community to which we belong."

The spirituality of the secular age will be oriented towards this amazing universe of which each of us is a tiny part, and towards our mystical relationship with the earth with all its living forms, human and non-human. It will be celebrated in a wide variety of rituals— indeed in any ritual that gathers people together into community and nurtures one or more of the following:

- An attitude of awe towards this self-evolving universe.
- An appreciation of the living ecosphere of this planet.
- An appreciation of the capacity of the earth to regenerate itself.
- The value to be found in life, in all of its diversity.

- An appreciation of the total cultural legacy we have received from our human forbears.
- Responsibility for the care of one another.
- Responsibility for the kind of planet we pass on to our descendants.

Such a spirituality could be called secular mysticism. It is not entirely new, for it is reflected in many insights from the past. One need only recall the almost hackneyed words of John Donne: "No man is an island entire of itself; every man is a piece of the Continent, a part of the main." And as far back as the ninth century that deep original thinker and great scholar John Scotus Erigena (c.810–877) was already addressing God as "the everlasting Essence of things beyond space and time and yet within them, the one who transcends and yet pervades all things."

A NEW WORLD, A NEW SPIRIT

In developing a spirituality for today's secular world we must not be primarily concerned with saving our individual selves, with self-improvement, with introspection, and least of all with any form of navel-gazing. Rather we must be primarily concerned for the welfare of one another, for the future of the human species, and for the health of the planet.

The spirituality of the secular world will evolve, if it evolves at all, out of the many cultures that have preceded it. It will be natural and not supernatural. It will be humanistic; first because it will need to serve all humanity, and second because it will be humanly based. In particular it will evolve out of the Christian past simply because the civilization of the Christian West indirectly caused the modern world to come into being.

But it will require the rise of a shared global consciousness—a consciousness of the human predicament, an appreciation of humanity's dependence on the earth, and a willingness to act jointly in response. Yet life is so precious and the evolutionary universe so mysterious that these should be more than enough to induce in us a sense of awe and joyful gratitude much like that which played a similar role in past religious experience. The religious rituals of the future will celebrate the wonder of the universe and the mystery of life. They will revolve around the natural processes that have brought life into being and continue to sustain it. All these things may be said to constitute the raw material of the spirituality of the secular age and the coming global culture.

In short, the spirituality of the secular age takes the form of the great coming together of all peoples on a global scale. The coming together will promote unity—unity and harmony among individuals, unity and harmony among the nations, unity and harmony with all forms of life, unity and harmony with the planet. Insofar as such spirituality needs some institutional structure it will be secular in character. For example, the United Nations, though already overdue for restructuring, is our current institution for nurturing unity among the nations. The various ecological movements form the institutions for nurturing the restoration of unity between the human species and the earth.

Just as the spirituality of the secular age cannot be restricted to any one particular set of rituals or institutions, so it cannot be fully expressed in any one language or formula. But if the God-talk of the monotheistic traditions were to survive, then we could say that the God being worshipped in secular spirituality is the connectedness of all that is. God—that is, the ultimate reality—is the oneness of the universe.

14

MOVING TOWARDS A NEW FORM OF MYSTICISM

EVERYTHING IN THE UNIVERSE IS CONNECTED

The Latin word from which we derive "universe" simply means "turned into one" and what turns "all that is" into a *universe* is connectedness. Of course what the ancient Romans understood as the universe has turned out to be only a small part of what we understand to constitute it. But even though we now believe the universe to contain galaxies far distant in space from our own, they are still connected and can all be traced back to a common origin that we currently call the "Big Bang." The phenomenon of connectedness is particularly germane when we consider our planetary home, the place that we call Earth. All life forms on this planet exhibit their own modes of connectedness, and we humans are part of this vast web. We are just as much creatures of the earth as are the wild animals and the insects. Metaphorically speaking, we have our roots in the earth just as much as plants and trees. We humans are made of the dust of the earth and to dust we return, as the Bible has long affirmed. Yet in the short interval that constitutes the life of each human, we are able to hold in our minds a mental picture of the whole universe. One of my favorite biblical authors observed this over two thousand years ago, when he wrote:

> Even the world itself God has put into the human mind,
> but in such a way that people cannot discover,
> from beginning to end, what it is that he has done.
> *(Ecclesiastes 3:11, c. 300 BCE)*

We need to pause for a moment to grasp the extraordinary fact that we are able to create in our minds a picture of the universe. It means that through us tiny earthly creatures the universe attempts, as it were, to look at itself. Unfortunately this fact has often had the effect of causing us to think we are beings *outside of* the universe— beings *apart from* of it. Then we cease to be aware of the connectedness of "all that is." A further unfortunate aspect of this amazing fact is that we too readily assume that the picture of the universe we hold in our minds corresponds exactly to the way things are. We fail to acknowledge that it is a picture we have constructed. Moreover, in the long and complex history of human cultures our predecessors have constructed many and often quite diverse mental pictures of the universe. Of course, the modern enterprise of empirical science makes us confident that our modern picture of the universe is considerably closer to reality than the many cultural pictures that preceded it.

I am going to suggest, however, that in some rather curious ways the ancients may have had a healthier understanding of the universe than we do today, and this in spite of the highly sophisticated technological culture of the west.

Fifty years ago, in 1958, I read a book entitled *The Intellectual Adventure of Ancient Man.* Written by five experts on the ancient Middle East, the cradle of Western civilization, it made some interesting points about how the ancients pictured the universe in which they found themselves and how they interpreted the forces of nature that they observed and encountered. Here are some of the conclusions they formed:

- Life permeates all that is, and this means that nothing is lifeless. Nothing can be designated "It": the whole universe is alive.
- Humans relate to the world (Nature) in the I-Thou mode, not as I-It. We relate to Nature in the same personal way as we relate to one another. We must listen to what Nature tells us and respond as Nature requires.
- Natural phenomena are willed by personal forces (gods and spirits).

Today we would say that without knowing it the ancients were projecting their own consciousness into what they observed in their world. This is how they came to create the widespread notion of spirits and gods. These supposed unseen spiritual beings were thought to inhabit all objects and phenomena in the known world. When the sun rose, the rivers flowed, or the storms descended, it was because these phenomena were alive and personal.

OUR LOST INNOCENCE

We can understand how natural it was to arrive at such an interpretation, for even today a two-year-old after accidentally hitting his head on a table corner will turn around and address the offending object saying, "You naughty table!" For people who concluded that natural objects were inhabited by spirits and gods, it was a simple step to imagine those unseen beings as not only inhabiting the rivers, mountains, and storms, but indeed as controlling them. To explain what we call natural phenomena, the ancients did not ask, "How did this event happen?" but "Who caused it—and why?" We should not be surprised, for as recently as this century large numbers of intelligent and nominally educated people expressed the opinion that the Indian Ocean Tsunami had been willed by God. In most ancient cultures it was believed that all natural phenomena reflected the will of the gods. Many of these societies envisioned a Sky Father and an Earth Mother who were the progenitors of all the other gods, each with his or her own portfolio or special area of operation.

Consider the example of pre-European Maori culture. Rangi is the Sky Father and Papa the Earth Mother. It was the embrace of these two that generated all the other gods, and it was Tane, the god of the forests and birds, who was finally successful in separating Rangi from Papa by pushing Rangi up into the sky by using the tall trunks of his trees. This further explained why the rain falls from above and the mists rise from the ground; they manifested the weeping of Rangi and Papa because they had been separated from each other.

In ancient Greece the name of the Earth Mother was Gaia. The word was often used poetically in place of *gē*, the Greek word for earth that has been preserved in our word for the study of the earth, "ge-ology." The male consort of Gaia was Zeus, the chief of the gods. Their counterparts in ancient Roman culture were Jupiter (the word even retains the word pater or "father") and his wife Juno. What we need to recall about both the ancient worldview and that of the continuing tribal cultures is that for these people all that exists forms a unity and constitutes.

ONE COMPLEX BUNDLE OF LIFE

Humans felt themselves to be within a vast and complex whole that was permeated by life. They saw themselves as part of a great variety of living forms, both visible and invisible, on which their own life depended. The gods, though invisible, were so immanent that ancient people felt themselves virtually living among these deities. How did we humans lose that sense of oneness? In the first millennium before the Christian era a radical cultural transition took place in Europe and Asia, a paradigm shift that did not reach the remote tribal areas of Africa, the Americas, and Australasia until much later. Karl Jaspers labeled this transition the Axial Period and defined its extent as a century or two on either side of 500 BCE. The transition was probably longer and more complex than Jaspers thought, but it nonetheless produced a radical cultural change. Karen Armstrong has called it *The Great Transformation* in her book of that title (Atlantic Books, 2006). Complex though this transformation was, and varying considerably in details from culture to culture, we can isolate certain broad common features if we compare the cultural situation before the Axial Period with that which obtained after it. What I here present here is an admittedly simplified description, but it should help us to understand some basic conceptual shifts of which we are the heirs.

A CULTURAL TSUNAMI

The Great Transformation brought a number of radical changes that affect the way we see and interpret reality (all that is) as distinct from the way both the ancients and tribal cultures did. The echo of the first of these changes can still be heard in the different ways that Europeans and Maori relate to the natural world. The Maori still feel a spiritual bond with the earth that Europeans do not. This difference can be traced back to the Great Transformation. It was then that for the first time in human consciousness there emerged the awareness of the purely physical or, to use Martin Buber's term, the It-world.

Whereas everything was once thought to be permeated by a life-force, a concept still preserved in certain Maori terms, during the

Great Transformation people came to recognize that some things in the world are not alive, nor have ever been alive. Not only are rocks and mountains not alive but neither are volcanoes, rivers, clouds and storms, however much movement and vitality they appear to show. The emergence of the It-world was a great breakthrough in human perception. In the long run it was destined to lead to the emergence of the physical sciences, especially physics and chemistry. The change is clearly illustrated in how astrology was replaced by astronomy. In astrology the planets were believed to be personal beings who determined human destiny; in astronomy they are objects whose movements can be measured and predicted. Today we so take for granted the difference between lifeless forms and living forms that we overlook the fact that our pre-Axial forbears did not recognize this divide. This basic difference between living and non-living plays a basic role in the game of 20 questions, in which one of the first determinations is "animal, vegetable, or mineral?"— the three categories into which we commonly divide all physical objects. The differentiation between lifeless and living forms was destined to lead to the reduction of the number of the gods, and much later to the elimination of all gods. Let us turn first to the reduction of the gods.

FROM POLYTHEISM TO MONOTHEISM

A second major change was that over a period of several hundred years the belief in many gods was replaced by the belief in only one God. Oneness became an important attribute of the divine or spirit world. "The Lord our God is One," says the Jewish Shema. In Islam, "Wahid" or "one" became one of the 99 beautiful names of Allah.

Why did this transition take place? The traditional answer is that the one true God spoke through such chosen prophets as Moses and Muhammad and dispelled the gods as unreal. But I suspect that human psychology had much to do with it. There is a correlation between the way we perceive our external world and the way we organize our internal world. Carl Jung described our mental growth to mature personhood as the process of individuation. It is a process by which each of us becomes by stages an integrated whole, a unified self. And that which happens quite naturally within our psyche, we unconsciously project onto the external world as we construct a picture of it. We experience a strong urge to establish order or unity out of the chaos of messages that our sense organs convey to the brain. It leads us to construct a *uni*verse, a turning of all that is into one. The accumulation of gods created in ancient cultures to explain natural phenomena at last became such a confusing jumble that the human psyche's innate search for unity demanded some means of unification.

We have a modern example in the way Isaac Newton's concept of gravity brought one simple explanation to three quite different phenomena: objects falling to the ground, ocean tides, and the path of the moon. The Greeks manifested this desire for unity in their use of the term "logos." The word means "human reason" and refers to the way our minds attempt to reconcile contradictions and resolve ambiguities. Our word "logical" derives from it. But "logos" was also the word the Greeks used to explain the underlying unity of the universe, as we see in the wonderful prologue of John's Gospel: "In the beginning was the logos and the logos was with God and the logos was God."

While we may offer a variety of theories as to why the transition from polytheism to monotheism took place, the fact remains that it did. And since most of the Bible was written during and after that transition, it documents the process very clearly. In it we can discern a battle being waged between the prophets who pioneered the emergence of monotheism and the defenders of polytheism who tried desperately to preserve the Canaanite worship of the forces of nature.

FROM THE SKY GOD TO A DUALISTIC UNIVERSE

As polytheism slowly evolved into monotheism, many of the features of the former Sky God were retained and transferred to the newly defined one and only deity. These included:

• His heavenly dwelling place (Our Father who art in heaven).

- His maleness (monotheistic traditions became patriarchal.)
- His almighty power as the storm god (now interpreted as divine anger).
- The disappearance of the Earth Mother. (All things feminine became degraded).

Furthermore, the immanence of the divine gave way to the notion of transcendence. Humans no longer imagined themselves living among the gods, but saw this as an earthly world far below the heavenly world in which God lived. And as one might perhaps predict, the physical world came in time to be not simply lower, but an inferior and even degraded place. When the overall unity of "all that is" was no longer sustainable, the one-world universe of the ancients became a two-world universe. After the Great Transformation this bifurcated reality was believed to consist of an unseen upper world (eternal and spiritual) and the visible lower world (materialistic, time-bound, and lacking spirituality) in which we live. And soon this lower world became a "fallen world," one wholly at the mercy of the spiritual world and destined for final destruction. Recall, if you will, both the gender balance among the pre-Axial gods and the fact that they lived in the same world as humans. After the great transformation the imagined world was a very different place.

THE CHANGES

- The earth becomes an It-world (material, non-living)
- The gods disappear.
- Natural phenomena are under the control of one God.
  ("I form light and I create darkness. I bring health and I create disease. I, the LORD do all these things."—Isaiah 45:7)
- Unusual natural events are "acts of God" (miracles).
- The sky is transformed into a new spiritual world.
- This spiritual world is seen as transcendent and eternal.

As this mentally constructed picture of all that is became increasingly dualistic, the eternal world began to expand and become more complex until, by the high Middle Ages, it completely dominated Christian consciousness. By 1400 CE the It-world no longer constituted the major portion of reality, but had become largely restricted to matters of biological survival: the spires of the great Gothic cathedrals pointed to the 'real', eternal world.

WE SHOULD NOTE THAT IN THIS NEW PARADIGM

- The earth has become a fallen world, doomed to destruction, and to be replaced at the end of time by a new heaven and a new earth.
- Heaven (the "city of God") has become increasingly populated with various kinds of spiritual beings.
- Fear of eternal punishment in the fires of Hell has become a dominant concern, with the milder ordeal of Purgatory a lesser but still worrisome threat.

Such was the eternal order of things created in the Christian imagination by the all-pervasive effects of Christian devotion.

But what has been humanly constructed in devout imagination can also fade away like a dream. The first change came during the Protestant Reformation, for in the Protestant world of 1500 CE Purgatory had disappeared. And by the late nineteenth century, many Christians could no longer reconcile the torments of Hell with an all-loving God. Its reality having been questioned and vigorously debated, Hell began to disappear from Christian consciousness. At the beginning of the twentieth century, then, even loyal churchgoers had a quite different picture of the world from that which had obtained less than a hundred years earlier. Though God and heaven remain, Hell is fast disappearing, and the earth, which is coming to be seen more positively, is looming larger in human consciousness. After all, by the end of the eighteenth century artists had begun to discover beauty in the landscape and think it worth painting, and the romantic poets of the early nineteenth century found their chief inspiration in the beauties of nature. It seems more than a coincidence that this same century saw the rise of secularism. The importance of the physical world could no longer be concealed by flights of supernatural fancy.

By the middle of the twentieth century the very idea of an afterlife was beginning to disappear from western consciousness, and God retained at best an uncertain existence. In the 60's, a number of theologians affirmed Nietzsche's dramatic announcement that "God is dead!" And what with the increasing popularity of panentheist and non-realist concepts of divinity, the reality of God may be compared with the grin on the disappearing Cheshire cat in Alice and Wonderland. At the beginning of the twenty-first century, then, we have had to accustom ourselves to a radically different picture of the real world.

SCIENCE'S NEW HEAVEN AND NEW EARTH

But is this all there is to it? Not by a very long way, thanks in large measure to Galileo. During the last four hundred years, as the dualistic world imagined by Christian consciousness has been slowly dissolving, another and much vaster picture of the universe has been replacing it. At the end of the nineteenth century astronomers were beginning to talk about an expanding universe; today we know that it is quite literally expanding and is so enormous that our minds can no longer contain it in the way our forbears thought they could.

Our world is a tiny planet in a solar system that revolves around a very average-sized star, one of some ten billion in the galaxy or star-cluster that we call the Milky Way. And ours is but one of ten billion such galaxies. Light from the sun takes less than *eight minutes* to get here, but that from the next nearest star travels *four and a half years* to arrive here. Light takes *500,000 years* to cross from one side of the galaxy to the other, but the distance to other galaxies must be measured in *millions of light years,* and our massive modern telescopes can now photograph the light they emitted long before our planet was formed.

From all this it should be obvious that the universe beyond our solar system cannot affect our daily life except as a matter of interest and curiosity. And pretty much the same is true of the rest of the solar system. But though it is an insignificant speck of dust in the context of the vast universe, planet earth means everything to us; for all practical purposes it constitutes our world. Not only has the unseen eternal world of heaven and hell vanished into unreality, but the "real" universe—the space-time continuum that replaced it—impinges on our daily lives even less than the imaginary former one did!

Now that the traditional heavenly dwelling place of God has been completely lost in the new picture of a universe that seems devoid of relevance for our lives, we might well feel utterly alone and deserted. What has happened to the God who replaced the gods at the Great Transformation?

"WHERE IS GOD TO BE FOUND?"

To deal with this difficult question, I shall borrow an idea from the philosopher Karl Popper. He suggested that to understand "all that is" in a way that does justice to human existence and to human knowledge, we should think of three worlds. They are very different from one another. The first is the physical world, World 1, which for us consists of the vast space-time universe. Through most of the universe's existence (as we now conceive it) nothing else but this physical world existed. But in the course of time, about three billion years ago, our planet Earth brought forth life, in the higher forms of which there evolved the phenomenon of consciousness.

This ability to become aware of the physical world through the medium of sensory experience produced a new, non-physical, non-spatial reality that Popper called World 2. It includes states of consciousness that range from the minimal perceptions found in simple life forms all the way to the critical self-consciousness of human beings. This latter potential emerged less than a million years ago, and though it is dependent on the physical brains of the human species, it is not, as Plato described the immortal soul, an independent entity.

In the course of time, however, the self-conscious reflection of humans on their personal and collective experiences created a third world, which is also non-physical and non-spatial. This World 3 contains language, the names of things, ideas, stories, religious beliefs, rituals, and the arts. In each human community this nexus became a body of continually growing cultural knowledge handed down from generation to generation. The idea of God belongs to this world, for it can now be seen to be a humanly created idea: it has evolved and changed within the complex body of cultural knowledge. In some cultures it has played a central role, while in others it has not. And eventually this third world gave rise to philosophy and science, which have in turn questioned the usefulness of the God idea. Furthermore, as it develops and changes, this third world also changes human consciousness and thus in turn affects the way humans understand and use the physical planet on which they live and of which they are a part.

Though invisible, World 3 is obviously of the utmost power and importance. Our very humanity arises from it, for each of us has been shaped by one of the cultural traditions that make up World 3. Through the accumulation of scientific knowledge World 3 has expanded at an exponential rate, far outstripping the capacity of one human mind to assimilate anything but a tiny fragment of its vast content. More than ever before we humans have become dependent upon one another, not only for the basic necessities of life but for the knowledge by which to live a satisfying life.

Further, World 3 is developing something like a life of its own, since through the mass media and the internet it is fast becoming available to people all around the world. In some respects World 3 may be said to have taken over the directive role once attributed to God. It speaks to us and challenges us with a kind of prophetic voice. If that seems an exaggeration or an untenable metaphor, consider this: At the present time the body of cultural knowledge (in World 3) is increasingly alerting our collective human consciousness (in World 2) to the fact that human activity in World 1 is having very serious effects on the ability of World 1 to sustain life in the same way it did in the past. In particular we are being warned that the earth cannot continue to support human life in the manner to which its affluent representatives have become accustomed.

CRUNCH TIME

Through most of human history, say the last 200,000 years, the human species had no real affect on the forces of nature. But the recent explosion of human population has changed this. The quadrupling of our numbers in the twentieth century and the world-altering power of modern technology have brought about unanticipated but grave perils. We are faced with food shortages, deforestation, increasing levels of pollution and carbon dioxide, global warming, changing weather patterns, rising sea levels, and deadly competition for oil. Yet just as World 3 is pointing out our responsibility for all life on this planet, it is also leading us to a discovery that may well be of vital importance—especially at a time when the traditional source of superhuman help is fast disappearing.

Consider the fact that up until only two to three thousand years ago, humans shared the world they lived in with a Sky Father, an Earth Mother, a throng of gods, and all the plants and animals of the ecosystem. Then, for the next two thousand years they lived in a three-tiered world that featured God with all his saints and angels up in a distant Heaven, Satan and all the damned relegated to the subterranean confines of Hell, and humans, animals, and plants here alone on Earth. But our present knowledge has redrawn the map, and the result is much like the original one—except that the imaginary figures have disappeared and we are left alone with the flora and fauna. What is perhaps a more important difference is that we now recognize that we bear a God-like responsibility for the preservation and welfare of all life on the planet.

To a great extent, in short, we have leaped backward into the future, and find that our understanding of our situation has much in common with that of the ancients.

- Earth has re-asserted its supremacy over humans.
- Earth is the mother of all life.
- Earth sustains all life.
- Earth can once again be called Gaia.

THE RESURRECTION OF GAIA

What is known as Gaia theory originated in the mind of an extraordinarily creative scientist named James Lovelock. At first he called it the Biocybernetic Universal System Tendency/Homeostasis. But as his friend and fellow villager, William Golding, author of *The Lord of the Flies* pointed out to him, "You need a more interesting name than that for something that seems so alive. I suggest you call it Gaia." So Gaia it became. In 1979 Lovelock wrote *Gaia: A New Look at Life on Earth*.

The Gaia theory proposes that the biosphere is connected with the other physical components of the Earth—the atmosphere, hydrosphere, and lithosphere—in such a way as to form a complex interconnected system. This web of being acts in a homeostatic fashion that operates so as to preserve the climatic and biochemical conditions on Earth that make it suitable for living systems.

Gaia theory does not say the earth *is* a living organism, but rather that life in all of its diversity has so evolved in relation to the physical forces of its earthly environment that its operation is *like* that of an organism—so much so that it is worthy of the name *Gaia*. Indeed, the living envelope of the earth and its environmental home together constitute a self-regulating system similar to the immune systems of the human body. For just as the human body has a remarkable capacity to restore itself to health or wholeness, so the natural forces of the earth have a remarkable capacity to preserve and restore the climatic and biogeochemical conditions on Earth that make it suitable for living systems.

DON'T FOOL WITH MOTHER NATURE!

We humans, particularly in the Western world, had come to assume the earth was an impersonal It. After the Great Transformation our cultural tradition led us to believe that we humans were a unique and god-like species, who had been given dominion over the earth and all of its other living forms. We believed that we could exploit the planet and its creatures for our own material advantage. World 3, which we ourselves have created, is now telling us we are suffering from hubris. We have overstepped ourselves. We have not paid sufficient attention to the natural forces of the earth. But now an enlightened concern for both our current well-being and the future welfare of all species—including our own—shows that we have ignored these forces at our peril.

Since the earth does not exist for us humans alone, then we dare not interfere too much with Gaia's homeostatic balance, lest we become like a cancerous growth. For in that case the natural forces that constitute Gaia may take action to eliminate our species in the same way as immune systems attack and destroy cancer cells. Immune systems do not think and plan, nor does Gaia—but the effect can be much the same.

REDEFINING SALVATION

Whether we adopt the Gaia model or not, the inescapable fact is that not only has human activity on this planet accelerated the extinction of many species, but it now endangers the future of our own species. The earth, now perhaps better understood as Gaia, is more responsive to our activity than we once thought. Indeed, the salvation of the earth and the salvation of our species have become one and the same goal. And since the concept of God may now be seen as a symbol for the responsibilities and virtues we feel bound to manifest, and since caring for the earth can now be seen as our supreme duty, then our traditional responsibility to God and our newly-found responsibility to the earth have become virtually the same.

What is more, we find that we humans, as creatures of the earth, are all part of Gaia. And as her most conscious element, our species now bears the responsibility to rediscover our essential connectedness with the earth, and thus to experience on the grand scale what individuals must strive to discover for themselves. We begin life in our mother's womb, physically at one with her. After our birth we are still physically dependent on the nurture we receive in the bosom of our family. But during adolescence our "programming" impels us to spurn parental authority, to distance ourselves from the security of family in order to become an independent self. In maturity, however, we learn to revalue our family and its connectedness, and to gratefully acknowledge our mystical origin.

In some respects the human species mirrors the individual: having passed through its adolescence and early adulthood, it now faces the challenge of achieving mature, responsible adulthood. Only as recently as the eighteenth century did we begin to acknowledge our common humanity and recognize its corollary emphasis on human rights and condemnation of racism. And though we have begun to outgrow a long history of tribalism we still have far to go and much to learn. Yet even before we have achieved the ideal of a common humanity, we are challenged to acknowledge our oneness with all life, our connectedness with the planet.

A "MYSTIC, SWEET COMMUNION"

This fresh awareness of our radical connectedness is giving rise to a new manifestation of mysticism. For the mystic, after all, is one who seeks by self-surrender to be united with, even absorbed within, the ultimate reality. Mysticism is a religious phenomenon that has surfaced in all the great religious traditions. Since theistic traditions thought of God as the ultimate reality, the mystic sought complete union with God. The Christian and Muslim traditions so magnified the transcendence of God that they frowned upon the aspirations of the mystics and often persecuted them. Mysticism flourished more in eastern traditions where deity was conceived more vaguely as the undefined spirit with which the human spirit has a natural affinity. To be sure, most traditional western forms of mysticism tended to assume the dualism of spiritual and material, and that had the effect of undervaluing the material. But modern understanding of human consciousness has replaced traditional dualism with a recognition of the unity of all reality, and this insight prepares the way for a new kind of mysticism.

Let me illustrate the point this way. The medieval Christian mystic Meister Eckhart said, "The eye with which I see God and the eye with which God sees me are one and the same eye." And now that we are learning to see ourselves as but one element of a living planet for whose future we have now become responsible, we can rephrase Meister Eckhart's aphorism in some such way as this:

> The eye with which I see Gaia
> is the eye with which Gaia sees itself.

As the aspiration of the mystic is to become one with ultimate reality, so the goal of the human race today must be one of abandoning all activities that have led us into an undeclared war with the planet while at the same time fostering and magnifying whatever endeavors will put us in harmony with the planet. One might even say that we have to recover the awe for Gaia that our ancient forebears had before the Great Transformation. It is indeed propitious that once again people are coming to see our planet home as Gaia, the Earth Mother that has brought us forth, nurtured us, and whom now we must honor and care for.

A PRAGMATIC MYSTICISM

This new form of mysticism is making its appearance wherever people evince a conscious concern for the care of the planet, and it is leading increasingly to such enterprises as conservation, environmentalism, sustainability, and protection of species. We may choose to use traditional God language of earlier mystics, or with some New Age mystics prefer the new Gaia language, or simply use the everyday human language of ecology—but in any case, we must now acknowledge, as did the ancients, that:

- We came from the earth.
- We remain creatures of the earth.
- The hope of our species for a viable future depends on our mystical re-union with the earth.

To celebrate this we might all do well to join in the Gaia song:
Gaia is the one who gives birth;
She's the air, she's the sea, she's Mother Earth;
She's the creatures that crawl and swim and fly;
She's the growing grass, she's you and I.

INDEX OF MODERN AUTHORS
AND THINKERS

ABOUT THE AUTHOR

S ir Lloyd Geering, ONZ, GNZM, CBE, is a public figure of considerable renown in New Zealand where he is in constant demand as a lecturer and as a commentator on religion and related matters on both television and radio. He is the lecturer for St. Andrew's Trust for the Study of Religion and Society, and Emeritus Professor of Religious Studies at Victoria University of Wellington, New Zealand.

Appointed to the Order of New Zealand in 2006, Geering was previously honored as *Principal Companion of the New Zealand Order of Merit* in 2001 and as a *Companion of the British Empire* in 1988. He is the author of several books including *Christianity without God* (2002), the precursor to *Coming Back to Earth*, and a trilogy of books—*Christian Faith at the Crossroads* (revised 2001), *Tomorrow's God: How We Create our Worlds* (reprint 2000), and *The World to Come: From Christian Past to Global Future* (1999).

In 1966, Geering published an article on "The Resurrection of Jesus" and, in 1967, another on "The Immortality of the Soul," which together sparked a two-year public, theological controversy that culminated in charges by the Presbyterian Church of New Zealand—of which he is an ordained minister—of doctrinal error and disturbing the peace of the church. After a dramatic, two-day televised trial, the Assembly judged that no doctrinal error had been proved, dismissed the charges and declared the case closed.

A documentary about the Lloyd Geering, entitled *The Last Western Heretic*, was broadcast on TVNZ in January 2008. It can be seen in its entirety on YouTube.

OTHER TITLES OF INTEREST FROM POLEBRIDGE PRESS

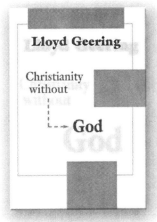

168 pages, paperback
2002 ISBN 0-944344-92-5

Christianity without God
Lloyd Geering

Could Christianity exist without belief in God? Before we can adequately answer that question, we must ask, What do we mean by Christianity? and What do we mean by God? In *Christianity without God*, Lloyd Geering explores those questions and their implications for the future of Christianity.

"My first reading of *Christianity Without God* was in a single day, as one might read a novel. It is that engaging and it reads as easily." —*Sofia*

192 pages, paperback
2008 ISBN 978-1-59815-010-0

When Faith Meets Reason
Religion Scholars Reflect on Their Spiritual Journeys
Edited by Charles W. Hedrick

What happens to faith when the creeds and confessions can no longer be squared with historical and empirical evidence? In the pages of *When Faith Meets Reason*, thirteen scholars take up the challenge to speak candidly about how they negotiate the conflicting claims of faith and reason.

"A slender book rich with large and profound ideas" —*Library Journal*

"This book could lead to a dangerous epidemic of honesty among religious thinkers." —*Richard Holloway, Retired Primus of the Scottish Episcopal Church*

Polebridge Press, Salem, Oregon
503-375-5323
503-375-5324 fax
877-523-3545 tollfree
www.polebridgepress.com

Free online study guide
www.faithmeetsreason.com

Breinigsville, PA USA
02 October 2009
225095BV00008B/3/P